SPIRIT RISING

Books by Jim Cymbala

Breakthrough Prayer
(book and audio)

The Church God Blesses
(book and audio)

Fresh Faith
(book and audio)

Fresh Power
(book and audio)

Fresh Wind, Fresh Fire
(book and audio)

The Life God Blesses
(book and audio)

When God's People Pray
(curriculum)

You Were Made for More
(book and audio)

JIM CYMBALA

WITH JENNIFER SCHUCHMANN

SPIRIT RISING

TAPPING INTO THE
POWER OF THE HOLY SPIRIT

ZONDERVAN.com/
AUTHORTRACKER
follow your favorite authors

ZONDERVAN

Spirit Rising
Copyright © 2012 by Jim Cymbala

This title is also available as a Zondervan ebook.
Visit www.zondervan.com/ebooks.

This title is also available in a Zondervan audio edition.
Visit www.zondervan.fm.

Requests for information should be addressed to:

Zondervan, *Grand Rapids, Michigan 49530*

Library of Congress Cataloging-in-Publication Data

Cymbala, Jim, 1943-
      Spirit rising : tapping into the power of the Holy Spirit / Jim Cymbala with
Jennifer Schuchmann.
         p. cm.
      ISBN 978-0-310-24125-6 (hardcover)
      1. Holy Spirit. 2. Christian life. I. Schuchmann, Jennifer, 1966-II. Title.
BT121.3.C97 2012
      231'.3—dc23   2011032038

Published in association with the literary agency of Ann Spangler and Company, 1420
Pontiac Road S.E., Grand Rapids, MI 49506.

Cover design: Extra Credit Projects
Cover image: Photos.com™
Interior design: Sarah Johnson

Printed in the United States of America

12 13 14 15 16 17 /DCI/ 20 19 18 17 16 15 14 13 12 11 10 9 8 7 6 5 4 3 2 1

To my late friend
Dave Wilkerson,
whose dependence on the Holy Spirit
in proclaiming the good news of Jesus Christ
was an inspiration to so many.

CONTENTS

FOREWORD

Every Sunday millions of people sit bored in church services. Even the churches that spend a fortune on production and put on a great show eventually dissatisfy. But think about something: Is it possible to be bored of the Holy Spirit? If He was truly moving, would we ever look at our watches? So ... isn't boredom a sure sign of the Spirit's absence?

This book is not about asking for the Holy Spirit's help. It is about asking Him to take over. It is for those who refuse to put up with going through the motions any longer.

"It is the Spirit who gives life. The flesh is no help at all" (John 6:63).

Stare at that verse. Do you believe it? Does your prayer life reflect it?

The Holy Spirit is not merely helpful. He is our only hope. He is the one who gives life. Yet when people lack life, the church often points to other solutions. When church services lack life, we grasp at so many other methods to try to generate excitement. This is not true at Brooklyn Tabernacle, where Pastor Jim has served faithfully for decades. Their solution for everything is prayer. And it shows.

One of the things I love about this book is that it is written by a man of God. Not a kid with a theory, but a man of God who has watched the Spirit work mightily during his many years of faithful ministry.

I remember, years ago, sitting at a conference and being amazed and a bit jealous as speakers impressed me with their knowledge and charisma. Then Pastor Cymbala stepped on stage. He was every bit as captivating as the others, but he spoke in such a way that I forgot all about him. He made me focus on Jesus. At the end of the sermon, I was in awe of God. I was focused on His word, not his.

It is clear from his teaching and writing that Jim Cymbala has an agenda: to make sure that Jesus is the only person glorified. While many "scholars" make every effort to assure us that we are not intelligent enough to understand the Scriptures without their help, Jim champions the ordinary person filled with the Holy Spirit. He encourages us to examine the Scriptures for ourselves in the power of the Spirit. He reminds us that it's all about Him, and He wants to empower, lead, teach, and use us. All of us.

We all see the problems in the church. We don't need another book to point those out. We now need the faith to believe that the solution really is that simple. The Holy Spirit.

—**Francis Chan**
Author of *Crazy Love*

Part One

GOD'S AGENT ON EARTH

[Chapter 1]

HOLY DISRUPTIONS

I wasn't expecting the Holy Spirit to join me for lunch, yet that's exactly what happened.

My wife, Carol, was out of town, so I went to a little café that I like on Long Island. I found a quiet table against the wall, ordered my usual salad, and while I was enjoying my healthy food, I caught up on some reading. I subscribe to the *New York Times* on my Kindle, and I'd already read through several stories when a headline caught my attention: "Hate Engulfs Christians in Pakistan." I was well into my salad by then, but I set my fork down as I read the article:

> The blistered black walls of the Hameed family's bedroom tell of an unspeakable crime. Seven family members died here on Saturday, six of them burned to death by a mob that had broken into their house and shot the grandfather dead, just because they were Christian.
>
> The family had huddled in the bedroom, talking in whispers with their backs pressed against the door, as the mob taunted them.
>
> "They said, 'If you come out, we'll kill you,'" said Ikhlaq Hameed, 22, who escaped. Among the dead were two children, Musa, 6, and Umaya, 13.[1]

The article described a rampage by a crowd of twenty thousand Muslims that lasted eight hours in Gojra, Pakistan, where Christians represent less than 5 percent of the population. In addition to the murdered members of the Hameed family, twenty Christians were wounded, and the mob burned and looted a hundred Christian homes, in some cases also wiping out the family's livelihood.

Why?

The day before, Christians at a wedding party in a nearby village were accused of burning a Qur'an. Officials who looked into the accusation said the charges were false, but local religious leaders used the news to rally Muslims against the local Christian minority.

The Hameeds, a Christian family, weren't involved in any of that. They were just eating breakfast in their home as the mob gathered nearby. When the grandfather opened the door to see what all the noise was for, the crowd of Muslims rushed inside. The Hameeds tried to take refuge in a back room as the mob entered their house and looted it before setting it on fire.

The Spirit Moves in Me

I couldn't believe what I was reading. Often the mistreatment of Christians goes unreported in the national media, but this story was in the *New York Times*. I searched other newspapers for additional information and learned that apparently Pakistani police had stood by while the carnage went on. A comment by one of the survivors moved me the most. He said he wouldn't retaliate because the Bible taught him to pray that his enemies would see the light.

I began to pray for the Christians in Pakistan, but as I prayed, I found myself weeping, and I had to turn my face toward the wall. I was concerned others in the café would see my tears and wonder what was wrong. What a tragedy! I couldn't imagine the suffering those people were going through because of their faith in Jesus. I felt such a bond with them — those brothers and sisters whom I didn't know personally but would one day spend eternity with.

Like Mr. Hameed, I am a Christian and a grandfather, but that's where the similarities end. I have never opened my door to an angry mob and tried to protect my family from looters. I've never watched my family die while trying to escape the flames of our burning house. I've never suffered physical violence because of my devotion to Christ. I could only try to imagine how those circumstances would test their faith. Or my faith.

Here in America, we believers may feel like our faith is being tested by something as silly as a traffic jam or a car that won't start. The truth is we're all spoiled, including me. I had so much and they had so little; our lives and experiences were worlds apart. And yet I now felt such a burden to help them. But how? I didn't know anyone in Pakistan. I was just a simple man eating lunch alone in a Long Island café.

The Holy Spirit had stirred my heart in an unusual way, and I couldn't cease praying for them. *Lord, be with your people. Help them to find food, work, a roof over their heads, and a bed where they can rest. Comfort them in their grief. Protect them. Guard their minds — don't let them lose faith because of the violence committed against them.* I prayed until I didn't know what else to pray. When I finished, I felt as if I'd done what I could, yet their tragedy remained in my heart like a weight.

For the rest of that Monday and most of the next day, I went about my business, but my mind frequently returned to those people, and each time it did, I interceded in prayer for them. One man had sold grain from a cart, but the mob had burned it along with a chest for his daughter's dowry. Where would he find work now that the tools of his trade were gone? Families were suddenly homeless and on the street searching for a place to live. The people in their church couldn't even help them, because a hundred other houses had also been burned and looted. Only God could help them cope with such pain and loss.

The Spirit Connects Two Worlds

Every Tuesday night the Brooklyn Tabernacle holds a prayer meeting. That next evening, as I sat in the front row singing and praying with my church family, I still couldn't get those Pakistani believers out of my mind. Something was unsettled in my spirit. I felt like I needed to do something more; I just didn't know what.

At some point in the meeting I stood up. "Something's heavy on my heart," I said to the church. "I can't shake this, and I want to share it with you. And then we're going to pray. I don't know what else to do." I pulled out my Kindle and prepared to read from it. "We're a long way from Pakistan, and most of us will probably never go there — but listen to this...."

As I read the article, I could feel the congregation's pain at the thought of a mother and her child being burned to death because of their faith. Like me, they grieved for those Christians who lost family members, homes, and jobs.

"Let's pray right now," I said after finishing the article. "God said in the day of trouble we should call upon him and he would answer us. Let's stand and get into groups of three or four all across the building. The Bible also says that the Lord is 'the God of all comfort.' Let's ask our Father to minister to those precious believers on the other side of the world." Immediately, fervent voices filled the building with the sacred sound of men and women calling on the name of the Lord.

I believe the Tuesday night prayer meeting at the Brooklyn Tabernacle is the spiritual engine that drives the church. My wife and I began there more than thirty-five years ago with a handful of people on Sundays and less than a handful on Tuesday nights. But now years later, at least fifteen hundred people were present. Some had come two hours early to get a head start at the throne of grace.

I joined hands with a few other men in the front row, and we added our voices to theirs. But as we finished praying out loud and I thought about transitioning into the offering, my mind was still searching for something else we could do. *Lord, we've prayed as best we could. Is there something else I am supposed to do? It's time for the offering; it would be great if we could send them some money. Maybe we can slice off a portion of tonight's offering to help these believers? But God, who would we send it to? I don't know anyone in Pakistan. I don't even know anyone who knows a Christian there. Should I mention this to the people? But what if I can't follow through on moving the funds to where they're needed? Oh God, direct me. Lead me to what I should do.*

I finished praying and moved back onto the platform. "Please be seated," I said.

As I paused, waiting for them to be seated, Craig, a leader in our church, rushed down the center aisle waving his hands to get my attention. I switched off my mike so I could hear what he had to say.

"Pastor, there's a woman sitting in the back — she's from Pakistan."

A woman from Pakistan in our downtown Brooklyn church on a Tuesday night? "Send her up," I told Craig.

Craig led her forward, and in front of everyone, with my mike still off, I chatted with the woman.

"Have you been here before?" I asked her.

"No, it's my first time."

"And you're from Pakistan?"

"Yes, my husband is a pastor there. My husband and my father-in-law were among the first outside Christians to go into Gojra to bring help."

"What?"

"Yes, they are there right now."

Just imagine, at that very moment, her husband was in the town we were praying for! He was working with other representatives to bring aid to the families who had lost loved ones and homes. That was her first time visiting the Brooklyn Tabernacle — the very same night I had spontaneously asked the church to pray for the Christians in Gojra, Pakistan.

I shared what she said with the people in the church. There was an audible gasp, and then the room filled with a sense of holy wonder and awe as people began to spontaneously thank God for this woman, her husband, and their ministry.

I was in shock.

The church was in shock.

The woman was in shock.

We had called out to God for some way to comfort and aid those involved in this catastrophe, and within minutes we found out the Lord was ahead of us.

> **We had called out to God ... and within minutes we found out the Lord was ahead of us.**

We took up a collection for the persecuted Christians in Pakistan, raising thousands of dollars for the Pakistani believers. I instructed Steve, our CFO, to check out the details of the woman's story and contact her husband. Everything was legit, and her husband seemed a very godly man. Later that week, another member of our church heard the details of what happened at the prayer meeting. He came forward and wrote a check for ten thousand dollars to add to what we had already collected. We sent the money to Gojra as quickly as we could.

Don't Miss the Blessing

Does that kind of story seem strange to you?

Have you ever been part of such a divine arrangement?

Perhaps you find the whole thing hard to believe. Maybe you even think it's the kind of story a pastor tells, embellishing the details for an effect. Or worse, perhaps you think I made it up.

But it happened.

And it shouldn't surprise us.

It was nothing more than the Holy Spirit leading a person, and then a church, to pray for and send help to hurting believers on the other side of the earth. No one had to think it up or figure it out — or for that matter, take credit for it.

Sitting in that café reading about the Christians in Pakistan, I felt a God-given burden for them even though I didn't know them. At the time, I had no idea what would take place in the next few days; I was just moved by their suffering and frustrated because I couldn't help. Now I understand why my heart had been so affected by their situation. If I had ignored the deep compassion for the Pakistanis that the Spirit had stirred in me, if I had ignored the prompting of the Spirit to pray, the connection that God had planned for that Tuesday night between our congregation and the Pakistani believers never would have happened.

What a loss it would have been if the people of Gojra had never received our financial aid. But what a bigger loss it would have been to me, and our prayer meeting, had we not experienced the working of the Holy Spirit in such a profound and dramatic way. God stepped in and did something "immeasurably more than all we [could] ask or imagine" (Eph. 3:20). He is that kind of dramatic, prayer-answering God, and we could have missed it. It was amazing to be a part of something so beautifully orchestrated and timed by the Holy Spirit.

But those kinds of Holy Spirit disruptions shouldn't seem shocking to us if we carefully read our New Testament. Examples of the Holy Spirit's work appear often in accounts of the early church. Unfortunately, today many of us have gotten used to doing without the powerful presence of the Holy Spirit working in our lives and churches.

Consider these honest questions:

- How many Christians suffer from a spiritual life that is dry and mechanical?
- How many serve a Jesus, whom they know about from the Bible, but who is not a living reality in their experience?
- And do we ever wonder why Holy Spirit interventions are so rare among our congregations?
- Could it be that we're missing out on some wonderful blessings planned for our lives and churches because we're not properly acquainted with the person and work of God the Holy Spirit?

The Holy Spirit is God's agent on earth, yet he is the least understood, least preached about, and least discussed member of the Trinity. And that is sad, because without him, our spiritual lives will always become a dry, mechanical struggle. That's why I am so happy you're beginning this study of the Holy Spirit. I can't think of anything else that will change your prayer life, your study of God's Word, and your experience during worship in church more than inviting the Spirit to join you in a new way.

> **The Holy Spirit is God's agent on earth, yet he is the least understood member of the Trinity.**

On the pages that follow, you'll learn more about who the Holy Spirit is, what happens when he moves, and how you can surrender yourself to his leading. Along the way, you'll meet some radically transformed people whose stories are so powerful I wanted you to hear them from the people who experienced them — in their own words and in their own chapters. There is only one thing more powerful than seeing the Spirit work in someone else's life, and that is seeing him work in yours.

If you want power, confidence, joy, peace, and more love in your life, ask the Spirit to come and do something new *in you*. Perhaps you'll be surprised when the Holy Spirit joins you for lunch, like he did me that day in that Long Island café. But I promise you that when he does, your spiritual life will cease to be dry and mechanical. Instead, it will be filled with awe at the power of the Spirit and the wonder of God's goodness.

Chapter 2

WHO IS THE HOLY SPIRIT?

Many Christians have only a vague notion of who the Holy Spirit is. They may have heard of him, but they struggle to understand his role. And some Bible translations haven't helped. The Holy Spirit isn't a "holy ghost" in the Halloween sense of a ghost. Neither is he a gas that fills up people, an ethereal presence, or a force like the one found in *Star Wars*.

The Holy Spirit is a real person — the third and coequal member of the Trinity. Though he is often overlooked or perhaps even neglected by many twenty-first-century believers, he is just as divine as the Father and the Son (Acts 5:3 – 4). Consider these facts:

- He possesses a divine personality and personally chooses people for ministry assignments (Acts 13:2).
- He communicates with us (Rev. 2:7) and searches out the deep things of God to make them known to believers (1 Cor. 2:9 – 12).
- He is the one who makes Christ a living reality to the believer (Eph. 3:16 – 17) and in fact is called the Spirit of Christ (Rom. 8:9).
- He is coequal with both the Father and Son as part of the mystery of the triune God.

Understanding these biblical facts about the Holy Spirit within the larger biblical story of who God is — Father, Son, and Holy Spirit — and how he relates to his people is important.

A Triune God

The triune God is a mystery that can't fully be explained. The Bible reveals God as a single God, one entity, who mysteriously exists in three persons — Father, Son, and Holy Spirit. Examining each of these three persons to more fully understand the Holy Spirit, the person who is the focus of this book, is worth a moment of our time.

THE FATHER

From reading our Bibles, we know that the Father, Creator God, is featured in the Old Testament. He is shown as the sovereign ruler of the universe. He is God the provider who faithfully answers prayer. He is also the Holy One of Israel who gave the Ten Commandments to Moses and to Israel — his chosen people. He knew the law would be a safeguard for them and bring blessings when obeyed. When Moses came down from the mountain and read the Ten Commandments, the people responded, "Everything God says to do, we will do." But unfortunately, they promptly started breaking every commandment they promised to keep.

Knowing the sinful tendencies of his people, God provided a sacrificial system for Israel as part of their worship. They offered sacrifices every morning and evening, including individual sacrifices, and most importantly, blood sacrifices. God had declared that without the shedding of blood there was no remission, or putting away of, sin. The only trouble with that sacrificial system was that their ongoing sinful tendencies resulted in endless sacrifices. Wherever the tabernacle was, and later in the temple itself, animals were brought in and slaughtered as a kind of temporary covering for their sins. But the blood of those animals could never cleanse their consciences, so the people were always living under a cloud of guilt and condemnation.

God had always planned an ultimate solution to the human sin problem.

God, however, had always planned an ultimate solution to the human sin problem. He promised that he would send the ultimate sacrifice one day, and this sacrifice would be in the Messiah. He would deliver the people of Israel from their sins, as well as anyone else who trusted in him. And God would send the Messiah at exactly the right time — on God's clock, not ours.

THE SON

The Son of God came to earth as a baby born to a virgin and was named Jesus. The New Testament records the wonderful story of his life, teachings, and miracles — works of power that demonstrated he was divine, the Son of God.

When Jesus came to earth, he didn't come just to teach and preach, or even to do miracles. He came primarily to *die*. For those Israelites and anyone else who violated God's laws (and that includes you and me), this was God's plan to rescue them from judgment. In Christian teaching, we often refer to this as "being saved from our sins," or *salvation*.

Salvation called for the Son to take on the guilt and suffer the punishment for our sins, past and present, so we would be freed from the condemnation of the law. Instead, Jesus would pay our sin-debt. That's why John the Baptist called Jesus the Lamb of God who would take away the sin of the world (John 1:29). A holy God can't punish twice for the same sin, so if Jesus Christ paid the price for our wanderings, law violations, and rebellion, we would never have to pay the price. Through the shedding of Christ's blood, God could forgive and forget our sins, and we would come into right standing with him. We would be "justified" — just as if we had never sinned.

It was a radical offer from God, and when Christ spoke of it, few people understood his meaning. Even the disciples, who had been with Jesus for years, couldn't comprehend God's plan of salvation. It wasn't until he appeared to them as the risen Savior that they began to understand what transpired when Jesus died on the cross.

One Problem

But still a problem remained. Even if Jesus washed my past from God's memory, even if everything I had ever done wrong was forgiven, what about today? What about tomorrow? What about when I am tempted to once again dishonor God and grieve Jesus who saved me from the consequences I deserved? In other words, where is the power to help me live differently than I did before? If I am going to be a new creation, then how? As grateful as I am to Jesus for washing my past clean, and as much as I desire to become like Christ in the future, I can tell you there is nothing that resembles Jesus Christ in Jim Cymbala. There is just no way I can be like him. A leopard can't change his spots. How could I ever change into a godly person and obey God's commands by my own self-effort?

But Jesus' death on the cross, as wonderful as that was, wasn't the end of God's plan. Before he died, Jesus told his followers about who else would be coming.

Jesus Promises to Send a Helper

During the Last Supper, Jesus told his disciples — the students who had learned from him and been friends with him for three years — that he was going away. Imagine how upset the disciples must have been to hear such a thing! He was their leader. He was a miracle worker. He was the one with the perfectly wise response when the Pharisees verbally cornered them. When he spoke, he spoke with an authority unlike any other teacher they had ever heard. No one had ever done that before.

How could he leave them? How could he leave them now, when they needed him most? And more confusing, he said that his leaving would benefit them. "But very truly I tell you, it is *for your good* that I am going away" (John 16:7, emphasis added).

That statement must have flabbergasted the disciples. How could it be *good* that Jesus went away? This was the teacher they had eaten with, walked with, traveled with, watched, and learned from. Any benefit from his leaving had to be impossible for them to understand.

Fortunately, Jesus explained the reason why. "I will ask the Father, and he will give you another advocate to help you and be with you forever — the Spirit of truth. The world cannot accept him, because it neither sees him nor knows him. But you know him, for he lives with you and will be in you" (John 14:16 – 17). Then again he said, "But very truly I tell you, it is for your good that I am going away. Unless I go away, the Advocate will not come to you; but if I go, I will send him to you" (16:7).

Now the whole picture began to unfold. The Father sent the Son to accomplish a specific work, to attest to God's love. "For God so loved the world that he gave his one and only Son, that whoever believes in him shall not perish but have eternal life" (John 3:16). God would show that love by sacrificing his Son on the cross to pay the penalty for our sins. And after the Son accomplished his work on the cross, rose from the dead, and ascended into heaven, the Son would send the Spirit.

After the Son accomplished his work on the cross, rose from the dead, and ascended into heaven, the Son would send the Spirit.

Although the disciples couldn't comprehend it at the time, it was better for them to have the invisible Holy Spirit *in them* than it was to have the physical Jesus *with them*. The divine person who was coming would help them understand everything he had said. But they would have to wait until Jesus returned to heaven before the Spirit would come.

THE HOLY SPIRIT

Acts 1 tells us that after Jesus rose from the dead, he spent forty days making appearances among the apostles and talking about the kingdom of God. Jesus also told them, " 'Do not leave Jerusalem, but wait for the gift my Father promised, which you have heard me speak about.... [And] you will receive power when the Holy Spirit comes on you; and you will be my witnesses in Jerusalem, and in all Judea and Samaria, and to the ends of the earth' " (vv. 4, 8).

They did as they were told, gathering in a house in Jerusalem to pray and worship God while they waited for the promise God made. "When the day of Pentecost came, they were all together in one place. Suddenly a sound like the blowing of a violent wind came from heaven and filled the whole house where they were sitting. They saw what seemed to be tongues of fire that separated and came to rest on each of them. All of them were filled with the Holy Spirit and began to speak in other tongues as the Spirit enabled them" (Acts 2:1 – 4).

Suddenly they received something from heaven, something that was far beyond their intelligence, talents, and training — the coming of the Holy Spirit in power. For the first time, they understood why it was good that Jesus went away. The Helper had come, and although Jesus was gone, the invisible Spirit had now taken residence in them and granted them power.

Perhaps the best way to understand what Jesus meant by saying it would be better for the disciples *after* he left is to look at the life of Peter. In the Gospels, Peter often spoke at the wrong time, misunderstood the meaning of Jesus' teachings, and tended toward boasting of his superiority over the other disciples. But when Jesus was arrested, Peter not only fled, but he also cursed and denied even knowing Jesus!

Why was Peter so weak and mistake prone?

How could Peter deny the Messiah who had selected him as part of his inner circle and worked countless miracles right before his eyes?

Didn't Peter have a gifted teacher? Yes, it was Jesus himself.

Did Peter lack a great role model and example to follow? No, he had the perfect role model in Jesus Christ in the flesh.

So then, what did all of those educational and inspirational resources do for Peter?

Not enough.

On the night Jesus was betrayed and arrested, Peter fled like everyone else.

With three and a half years of excellent discipleship under his belt, Peter learned the harsh truth we all have confronted — it's one thing to know the Word, but it's quite another to obey it. Even the best discipleship training and spiritual accountability proved insufficient for Peter, because *no outward teaching* can compare to the *inward power of the Holy Spirit.* If you need proof, look at Peter on the day of Pentecost when the Spirit was poured out. Though the political climate hadn't changed from the time Jesus was arrested and crucified, Peter now preached boldly about the name of Jesus to massive crowds. This was a new Peter! He was filled with the Spirit. Jesus' promise about the Holy Spirit's power was right there to see in Peter's life. Suddenly that failed disciple was preaching with such amazing effectiveness that thousands converted to Christ. Jesus had been *with* Peter, but now the Spirit was *in* him.

If we follow Peter's story through the book of Acts, we see him continuing to act with wisdom and courage. He was a different man. Jesus' words had come to fulfillment: "But very truly I tell you, it is for your good that I am going away" (John 16:7). Through his physical body, Jesus could be a mentor, teacher, preacher, and friend to the disciples, but he couldn't produce change from the inside out. This would be for the Spirit to accomplish just as God had planned from all eternity.

The Birth of the Church

The Christian church was born through the power of the Spirit. As we read through the rest of the book of Acts and the epistles of the New Testament, we see a picture of the early church the way God intended it to be. "They devoted themselves to the apostles' teaching and to fellowship, to the breaking of bread and to prayer" (2:42). Here was a community of believers who freely loved the Word of God and were devoted to the apostles' teaching. No one needed to badger or coerce them to love the Word. Instead, the Spirit within them inspired it. The same Spirit who wrote the Bible created an appetite inside of them for what it said. They shared with one another the deep love the Spirit had put in their hearts. They also became bold witnesses for Christ, filled with wisdom beyond their training. Their hearts were full of the Holy Spirit, and they experienced surprises as God did things that no one could anticipate.

The same Spirit who wrote the Bible created an appetite inside of the believers for what it said.

Not only had the Holy Spirit been sent to earth, but he was also *moving*. He acted in and through his people — he demonstrated his power to glorify Christ. The early church experienced him moving in their hearts and in their lives. Because of the hostile environment around them, they were repeatedly driven back to God for a fresh supply of the Holy Spirit, and they were wise enough to yield to his direction. Is the Holy Spirit moving like that in our lives? And in our churches?

Many people find it easy to relate to God the Father and Jesus the Son, but when it comes to the role of the Spirit in their lives, they don't have a clear picture of who he is or what he does. Do you ever feel that way? What about your life and your church? When you read about the power of the Holy Spirit in the life of Peter and in the early church, did it remind you of your own experience of the Holy Spirit? Or did you find yourself longing for something more?

I sometimes wonder, if the early Christians were around today, would they even recognize what we call Christianity? Our version is blander, almost totally intellectual in nature, and devoid of the Holy Spirit power the early church regularly experienced. How much loss do we suffer because we don't expect the Spirit to show up as promised? Everything we read about the church in the New Testament centered on the power of the Holy Spirit working in the hearts of Christian believers. Sadly, for many of us, this has not been our experience.

I believe it's time to return to the kind of faith we see in the New Testament church. They believed in Christ's word, they expected the Spirit to do great things, and he came through as promised.

He will do the same for us today.

Chapter 3

CHRISTIANITY IS HOPELESS WITHOUT THE SPIRIT

The world is full of books about God the Father who created the universe, and more books are written about Jesus the Son of God than anyone who ever walked on this planet. But isn't it interesting that far fewer books have been written about God the Holy Spirit?

When teaching on prayer, Jesus declared; "If you then, though you are evil, know how to give good gifts to your children, how much more will your Father in heaven *give the Holy Spirit* to those who ask him!" (Luke 11:13, emphasis added). You would think that promise would create a huge desire to know more about this promised Helper — who he is and what he does. And it would be even better if we were to experience him as a living reality the way the early believers did.

We know that Jesus the Son is seated at the right hand of the Father (Luke 22:69; Eph. 1:20; Col. 3:1). So that means the Holy Spirit is God's only agent on earth. He is the only experience we can have of God Almighty, the only way we can have the work of Jesus Christ applied to our lives, and the only way we can understand God's Word. Without the Holy Spirit, we are like the disciples before Pentecost — sincere but struggling with confusion and defeat.

More than a hundred years ago, Samuel Chadwick, a great Methodist preacher and leader in England, summed it up concisely: "The Christian religion is hopeless without the Holy Ghost."[1]

The early church provides the perfect illustration of that hopelessness. It was made up of simple men and women. The leaders were former fishermen and tax collectors who fled in fear when Jesus was arrested and needed them most. They weren't courageous and faithful. In fact, they *lacked* faith and courage. They were the least likely to be put in charge of any Christian enterprise.

Yet after the events in Acts 2, when the Holy Spirit is poured out, those same nobodies were suddenly transformed. With courage and faith, they turned their community, and eventually the world, upside down. That wasn't due to their seminary training; they didn't have any training. They couldn't hand out copies of the New Testament, because it hadn't been written yet. It wasn't because they were wealthy and had the greatest sound system and light show at their church. They were poor people without a church building. In fact, the Christian church didn't get its first public building for about three hundred years. To the existing Jewish religious establishment, those early Christians were mocked as unlearned and ignorant people with few resources. To the Roman Empire they seemed fanatical and strange.

But one thing they did possess was the power of the Holy Spirit. Jesus told them to rely on the Spirit for everything, including impromptu speech. To paraphrase, he said, "Don't even prepare what you'll say when you're in high-pressure situations, because when you open your mouth, it will be given to you. The Father will give it to you through the Holy Spirit. You'll just know what to say" (Mark 13:11). The early believers knew all too well that Christianity was hopeless without the Holy Spirit.

Giving the Holy Spirit His Due

The Holy Spirit is underappreciated and underpreached by the twenty-first-century church. There is a prejudice of sorts against the Holy Spirit that impedes many from learning more about him. The body of Christ is often divided into two sides. One side stresses the Word of God, separating itself from what it views as the emotional fanaticism often linked to those emphasizing the work of the Holy Spirit. The other side is sometimes known for drifting into unbiblical manifestations and unorthodox teaching while attributing it all to the Spirit of God.

Seeing the abuse and bad teaching, many on the first side will say, "I'm not interested in experiences and manifestations of the Holy Spirit. I just want to study the Word." But it was the Holy Spirit who inspired the Bible, and there are lots of promises concerning his person and work. How can anyone treasure God's Word without giving the Holy Spirit his rightful place?

To those who move in circles strongly emphasizing the Holy Spirit, they must be reminded that *everything* must be tested by Scripture. The Spirit never contradicts the Word he gave us. He also never puts the focus on the preacher, because the Holy Spirit was sent to glorify Christ alone (John 16:14).

Somewhere in the middle is the kind of Christianity we see in Scripture where the Word of God is honored along with a childlike dependence and openness to the Holy Spirit.

Only the Holy Spirit can make the things of Christ real and alive to people. Christianity does not stop at the cross where Jesus died and paid the price for our sins. After Good Friday was Resurrection Sunday when the Spirit raised Christ. Yet so many of us live with faint trickles and shallow pools of the Spirit, rather than the promised rivers of living water. "On the last and greatest day of the festival, Jesus stood and said in a loud voice, 'Let anyone who is thirsty come to me and drink. Whoever believes in me, as Scripture has said, *rivers of living water* will flow from within them.' By this he meant the Spirit, whom those who believed in him were later to receive. Up to that time the Spirit had not been given, since Jesus had not yet been glorified" (John 7:37 – 39, emphasis added).

> **Only the Holy Spirit can make the things of Christ real and alive to people.**

Everything about the Spirit speaks of powerful currents of life that refresh us and flow out to bless others. But there is an even more extraordinary teaching about the Spirit. Paul wrote, "If the Spirit of him who raised Jesus from the dead is living in you, he who raised Christ from the dead will also give life to your mortal bodies because of his Spirit who lives in you" (Rom. 8:11). Imagine, the measuring stick of the power promised to us is the same strength that raised the corpse of Jesus Christ from the dead!

Only the Holy Spirit

Let's remember how any person becomes a Christian. Before a person can feel the need for Jesus Christ as a savior, that person must first be convicted of sin. "When [the Spirit] comes, he will prove the world to be in the wrong about sin and righteousness and judgment" (John 16:8). The Holy Spirit shows us our sin and our need for a savior. That is what every believer experiences in conversion to Christ.

Jesus also taught that entrance into the kingdom of God (being "born again") can only happen by the Holy Spirit's work: Jesus told Nicodemus, "Very truly I tell you, no one can enter the kingdom of God unless they are born of water and the Spirit" (John 3:5).

Consider the insightful words of R. A. Torrey, evangelist and Bible teacher:

> The Holy Spirit does regenerate men. He has power to raise the dead. He has power to impart life to those who are morally dead or decaying. He has power to impart an entirely new nature to those whose nature now is so corrupt that to men they appear to be beyond hope. How often I have seen it proven. How often I have seen men and women utterly lost and ruined and vile come into a meeting scarcely knowing why they came. As they have sat there, the Word was spoken, the Spirit of God has quickened the Word thus sown in their heart, and in a moment, that man or woman, by the mighty power of the Holy Spirit, has become a new creation.[2]

It is the Holy Spirit working inside of us that causes us to turn from our sin and fix our eyes on Jesus. While we may be tempted to think that we can create emotional environments for this to happen, the truth is that this kind of rebirth or transformation can happen only through the work of the Holy Spirit.

The apostle Paul taught that believers are "temples of the Holy Spirit" (1 Cor. 6:19), and because the Spirit lives inside of us, that makes us different from the rest of the world. If the Holy Spirit doesn't live inside a person, no church membership or even a sincere effort to live a good life can make that person a Christian. Only true faith in Jesus Christ as Savior, confirmed by the Holy Spirit living inside of us, makes us a new creation. The Spirit inhabiting every believer is just another way of saying "Christ in us," for the Holy Spirit's presence represents Jesus.

When God looks down on the earth, he doesn't focus on ethnicity, and he never acknowledges religious denominations. He just sees two kinds of people; his children who have the Spirit living inside of them and unbelievers who don't have the Spirit living inside of them. It's as simple as that. Today we split hairs about doctrinal positions to validate our faith, but to the early church the definition was simpler. Either we are temples or we are not temples. "If anyone does not have the Spirit of Christ, they do not belong to Christ" (Rom. 8:9). It would have been impossible for the apostles to consider someone a true believer in Jesus without the accompanying witness and work of the Spirit. The Spirit of God was the bottom line.

It would have been impossible for the apostles to consider someone a true believer ... without the work of the Spirit.

Gojra Continued

Remember the story of the Pakistani believers whose homes had been looted and burned, and how the wife of the minister helping them showed up in our prayer service? Well, the story doesn't end there. The Spirit wasn't done with what he wanted to accomplish.

Months later on a Saturday night, I got a call from our CFO.

"The minister from Pakistan just called. There's a problem now in his city."

"What's wrong?" I asked.

"At the five o'clock Muslim call to prayer, something set them off. Now they're shouting, 'Death to the Christians! Burn their houses down. Death to the Christians!' He's really concerned."

"Okay, I am going to pray tonight. You pray too, Steve. What else can we do? Let's just pray."

So I prayed that night.

Before each of our three services, I always meet with the Prayer Band. They are a group of committed believers who pray with me and then gather together in a room to intercede for the attendees in each service. Our first Sunday service started at nine o'clock, and by the time I finished praying with the Prayer Band, the meeting had already started. I pushed the button for the elevator to go down to the sanctuary, and when it opened, Steve was in the elevator. He held his cell phone, and I could tell by the look on his face that something was wrong.

"He just called again. The situation's worse. He's up on the rooftop with his wife and children and some of the local Christians. There are thousands of people in the square chanting, 'Death to the Christians!' I can hear the fear in his voice and the chanting mob in the background, so I know what he's saying is true."

I felt as if I'd taken a punch and the air had been knocked out of me. I didn't know what to do. I got into the elevator, and we headed down. As we walked into the sanctuary, the congregation was singing and praising God. When the song ended, I interrupted and told the congregation, "We're going to get back to worshiping God in a moment, but right now there is an emergency situation we have to pray about."

I told the church what I knew. As I relayed the critical situation, my heart burst as I thought about parents and children hiding out on the roof from the crowd below. Then I broke down as I thought of what it would be like to be up there with my children and grandchildren. Overcome by emotion, I asked our worship leader Onaje to lead the church in prayer. Suddenly a chorus of cries went up to God on behalf of the Pakistani believers. It was just like what occurred in the book of Acts: "They raised their voices together in prayer to God" (4:24).

At the end of a long day, I spoke to Steve and asked what happened.

"You won't believe this," he said. "The pastor called me back."

"He's okay?" I was thrilled. The situation had been so dire.

"As they were on the rooftop, some clouds came out of nowhere. It got dark and started to rain, but not just rain, a torrential downpour. It rained so hard it dispersed the crowd! Everyone was safe, and they were able to get off the roof and return to their homes."

"Oh, thank you, Jesus! Praise God!" I couldn't wait to tell the church. God rescued the man, his family, and the other local Christians through the prayers of his people half a world away. Didn't God promise that praying to him in faith would bring answers from heaven?

The Holy Spirit was working in Pakistan, protecting those believers from the mob. But at the same time, the Holy Spirit was also moving among the people of our church, helping them to pray fervently and with a bold faith that only God could give.

Genuine Holy Spirit Manifestations

To many people this story about Pakistan might seem "out there." But maybe that's because without the Spirit of God moving strongly among us, many of us have become faithless and cynical. We have seen so much ministerial self-aggrandizement and so many dubious financial appeals linked to a supposed "Holy Spirit anointing," that we have turned away in disgust because so little reminds us of Jesus.

But don't the false appeals prove that something true really does exist? William Booth, founder of the Salvation Army, said, "We are not such fools as to refuse good bank notes because there are false ones in circulation; and although we see here and there manifestations of what appears to us to be nothing more than mere earthly fire, we none the less prize and value, and seek for the genuine fire which comes from the altar of the Lord."[3] The counterfeit proves there must be a true genuine manifestation of the Holy Spirit! There is a counterfeit gospel, but there is also a true message of salvation. There are false portrayals of Jesus, but there is also the true Son of God, Savior of the world. And so it is with the Holy Spirit. We must not be scared away by the abuses.

To the Corinthians, Paul said: "Now to each *one* the manifestation of the Spirit is given for the common good" (1 Cor. 12:7, emphasis added). There it is staring at us. Now what are we going to do with this verse? The infallible word of God says the *manifestation of the Holy Spirit* was given to each one for the common good. To each one, not just to the apostles. Think of the impact of that verse. Is that something we preach? Do we believe it? Do we pray about it? Do we expect it? God has promised every one of us a manifestation — supernatural by definition — of the Holy Spirit. It is part of being a Christian. To water that down to mean human talent is unbelief in God the Holy Spirit.

God has promised every one of us a manifestation of the Holy Spirit. It is part of being a Christian.

One of the ways the Spirit glorifies Christ is to build up his body for the common good. That is how God strengthens his church. Since the church is a spiritual organism, it needs spiritual ministry to build it up. Spiritual ministry can only come by the Holy Spirit showing himself through human beings. His power flows through human vessels.

Don't you agree that those who engage in false displays and teachings of the Spirit have scared away many sincere people who love their Bibles? Someone who truly loves the Word of God sees those displays and says, "No, thank you. Let's just have some safe praise singing and a good Bible study, and then we'll go home." But our Lord Jesus Christ never intended that *his* church operate without visitations and blessings from the living Spirit of God. Why would he send another Helper if not to help us? Just look around at our world. Don't we see the obvious need of something fresh from God to overcome the powerful influences of evil?

The early church was alive and active because of the Holy Spirit. There is no verse — *not even one* — that relegates the importance and vitality of the Spirit only to the New Testament church. That's the key — we have to believe the Holy Spirit is present for us today. We can only receive according to our faith. If we don't believe, we won't pray, and when we don't ask, we won't receive the blessings God has for us.

If we want to see God work in extraordinary ways, we have to follow the promptings of the Holy Spirit — just as I did in that café when I wept over people I didn't know, and just as the church did the night the wife of the Pakistani minister came forward.

Torrential rain came and helped those believers on the roof. We too need rain, but of another kind. Oh how easy for us to become parched and dry. What we need are fresh showers of blessing to soften our hearts and to bring fruitfulness to our lives. That's why the Old Testament prophet cried to God, "Rend the heavens and come down" (see Isa. 64:1, 3).

Come down on us, Holy Spirit, for we are truly helpless without you.

Chapter 4

CONTROLLED BY THE SPIRIT

We all have influences in our lives. The way we think and dress, and even the goals we set, have been shaped by various influences over the course of our lives. Some of those influences have become deeply embedded in us, while others we have rejected. But the fact is, we are all a product of multiple influences.

Occasionally, however, something that started as one of many contributing influences becomes more dominant and perhaps even begins to subtly control us. This control can powerfully shape our personalities — the way we see things and the way we react to situations. We all have met folks who respond to the world through the control of things such as drugs, alcohol, money, obsessive thoughts, weight issues, failed dreams, or fear. When an idea, a substance, or another person controls us, it affects nearly everything we do. A Christian counselor who understands what or who controls a person can help that person to focus on the problem.

Recently I was in the bank waiting to finish my transaction. The teller at the window next to me motioned for the next person in line to approach. The man who was waiting stomped to her window, muttered something under his breath, and slammed his paperwork on the counter.

"Your stupid ATM isn't working!" he said loud enough for everyone to hear.

The teller assumed that it was the one outside the bank. "I'm sorry, sir. We'll have someone go out and take a look at it."

"No! It's that one!" he said, pointing at the machine near the door. "That one right there! See it? Right there!" He kept pointing, making himself look ridiculous. A woman with a stroller crossed in front of the machine, and he yelled, "Get out of the way! Otherwise she still won't see it, and it'll never get fixed!"

As I looked around, his seething anger seemed to have affected everyone within earshot. Something had obviously happened before he went to the bank, minutes, hours, or maybe even years before, something totally unrelated to the troublesome ATM. But now he was completely controlled by anger.

We have all known people like him. They suffered a slight or even a grave injustice in the past, and they became infuriated. They never dealt with their rage and never resolved it. They spent the rest of their lives increasingly controlled by that anger. If they went out to eat, they were angry when they ordered. They were angry when they talked about their past and angry when they looked into their future. In some cases, their anger affected their spouses or their children until all those around them were painfully scarred or developed their own anger issues.

In the next chapter, you'll read Roma's story. Roma is a member of the Brooklyn Tabernacle; he grew up in Harlem in the 1970s, and what he saw happening on the streets heavily influenced him. Some of those influences, such as drugs, alcohol, and greed, ended up controlling him. But he also had other influences in his life fighting against all the negativity he encountered on streets, including a mother who prayed for him, a brother whom he looked up to, and the movies that helped him to escape the street life for a few hours a week. As Roma tells his story, you'll see that he had to make choices about all those influences. He had to choose what would control him, and as he'll tell us, he didn't always make the best decisions.

Good influences are gifts from the Lord and help us develop into the people he wants us to become.

You and I are just like Roma — we have been influenced by people and experiences. We didn't grow up in a vacuum. Our personalities weren't shaped on a deserted island. That's why it is so important to make sure we have godly influences in our lives, that we are surrounded by good people. Good influences are gifts from the Lord and help us develop into the people he wants us to become.

But here's the thing: regardless of whether we have had good influences or bad influences, we still get to decide what will influence our future. It is heartbreaking to meet people who instead of seeking God's strength during the battles of life, have become hardened, embittered, unforgiving, and cynical. You probably know some people like that. You say to them, "Hey, what a beautiful day," and they answer with, "Well, it's not gonna last long." The glass is always half empty, and negativity is the air they breathe. Those people didn't start life that way. They weren't born that hardened. Somehow they have let the negative influences in their lives control them.

Moving In and Making a Home

As Christians, our lives have been purchased for a price, and we now belong to God. The price was the blood of Jesus Christ, which he shed on the cross. Just as Israelites in the Old Testament belonged to God through covenant, Christians belong to God through the salvation we have experienced. We're God's people now. We belong to him — rescued out of the clutches of sin, guilt, and condemnation, and adopted into his family. In this case, being bought and owned by someone isn't a negative thing; it's a beautiful thing.

God saved us for the purpose for making us human temples, inhabited by his Spirit. During Old Testament days, God dwelt within the inner room of the temple — a place called the Holy of Holies. That's where he made his home. When Paul said Christians were the "temples of the Holy Spirit" (1 Cor. 6:19), the word he used for "temple" was not the word used for the outer rooms of the Old Testament temple. It was *naos*, which referred to the inner sanctum, the place where there was a visible manifestation of the *shekinah* glory of God.

That indwelling of God through the Holy Spirit makes Christians different from any other religionists on earth. Judaism, Islam, and Buddhism — none of these religions claim that their god inhabits their followers. The leaders of those belief systems may try to proselytize with their doctrine, but the gospel of Christ is different. Faith in Jesus makes us walking miracles who have been changed through the Holy Spirit personally dwelling in us!

God's plan in redemption was that we should live life *full* of the

Holy Spirit. "Do not get drunk on wine, which leads to debauchery. Instead, be filled with the Spirit" (Eph. 5:18). The metaphor here is that we might be filled with the Spirit to the point where he over-flows — spilling out onto others with love and grace. That's a beauti-ful image, isn't it? But it's not the clearest explanation of the Holy Spirit's relationship to the believer. When you consider that the Holy Spirit is a person, the third person of the Godhead, what does it mean to be *filled* with a person? He's not a gas. He's not a liquid. He's as much a person as the Father and the Son. So I think a better descrip-tion of "being filled" is to say the Spirit *controls* us.

Sadly, there are too many believers today who profess faith in Christ but who haven't surrendered themselves to the control of the Spirit. I am the last person who wants to get into a doctrinal dispute, and I understand that Christians have varied opinions. But because of the urgency of the hour and the state of affairs in our churches, I think we must look at the obvious difference between Christians who are born again and those who are living a Spirit-controlled life.

Controlled by the Spirit: A Biblical Imperative

The Bible shows us the importance of living a Spirit-controlled life. Taking a look at the passages in Acts 6 and Revelation 3, we can see the importance of going deeper with God.

EVEN EARLY CHURCH WAITERS NEEDED THE SPIRIT

In Acts 6 the apostles had to choose what many have come to call the first deacons. There was a dispute between the Grecian Jews and the Hebraic Jews about the fairness of the food distribution system. The apostles decided to appoint some men to handle that task so food distribution would get proper attention while the apostles continued to focus on "prayer and the ministry of the word" (v. 4).

The apostles said, "Brothers and sisters, choose seven men from among you who are *known to be full of the Spirit* and wisdom" (v. 3, emphasis added). Handing out food was a straightforward menial task, yet the apostles felt that being full of or controlled by the Spirit was a necessary qualification to wisely handle that simple job.

Compare that with some of our contemporary church hiring practices. When selecting people for professional ministry positions, we usually look first for educational qualifications. Folks who have earned a seminary degree become prime candidates to lead Christ's people without anyone having first discerned whether these potential leaders show evidence of being controlled by the Spirit. Then candidates are often given a battery of psychological tests to see if they're compatible for ministry, as if science were the deciding factor on wisdom. But in the New Testament church, even the job of distributing food to widows required leaders who were Spirit-controlled and full of wisdom.

> **In the New Testament church, even distributing food to widows required leaders who were Spirit-controlled and full of wisdom.**

Earlier, I mentioned R. A. Torrey, who was an outstanding evangelist. In 1899 he was chosen by D. L. Moody to be the first president of Moody Bible Institute in Chicago, which educates people for ministry. Given Torrey's unique experience as an educator, it is interesting to read this:

> We think that if a man is pious and has had a college and seminary education and comes out of it reasonably orthodox, he is now ready for our hands to be laid upon him and to be ordained to preach the Gospel. But Jesus Christ said, 'No.' There is another preparation so essential that a man must not undertake this work until he has received it. "*Tarry* [literally 'sit down'] ... *until you are endued with power from on high*"[1] (Luke 24:49).

If all believers were full of the Holy Spirit, if everyone in the community were Spirit-controlled, the apostles wouldn't have laid down such a qualification. In fact, it would be downright silly. Imagine them saying, "Choose seven people who are breathing." Being a Christian does not necessarily guarantee that a person lives a life controlled by the Spirit. The example above is further illuminated in a love letter Jesus sent to some believers two thousand years ago.

A LUKEWARM CHURCH

In Revelation 3, Jesus spoke to the church at Laodicea. This was a Christian church — one of the golden lampstands in that prophetic picture. These were Jesus' people. Yet he said to them, "I know your deeds, that you are neither cold nor hot. I wish you were either one or the other! So, because you are lukewarm — neither hot nor cold — I am about to spit you out of my mouth" (vv. 15 – 16).

We're not sure what Jesus meant by hot or cold. We do know (and we'll discuss in a later chapter) that one of the symbols of the Holy Spirit is fire, and of course, fire is hot. It's easy to imagine how a Spirit-controlled church could be "on fire." And we can picture that cold means the opposite, absolutely no evidence of the Holy Spirit, no fire, no flame. But this church was neither hot nor cold. They were just lukewarm, and Jesus was about to spit them out of his mouth because of that.

Now if some are compelled by their doctrinal position to insist that the Laodicean Christians were actually *full of the Holy Spirit* — because they insist that to be a Christian is automatically to be filled with the Spirit — then what they are saying is this: Jesus was vomiting Spirit-filled, Spirit-controlled believers out of his mouth. If that's the case, then lukewarmness means nothing and the words of Scripture become meaningless.

When we look at the Christian landscape today, we see many churches that are doing great things for God — people are finding Christ and being baptized, prayer meetings are bringing down God's blessings, and a spirit of love is pervading the atmosphere. The Spirit of Christ is in those churches, and excitement is in the air.

But we also can see some churches that probably give Jesus Christ a bad name. They're lukewarm. They dishonor the Lord because of their actions and attitudes. The pastor might preach biblical sermons, but there is scant evidence of God's unconditional, tender love and little sense of God's Spirit. The inevitable signs that God's Spirit is in control are absent; in fact, a deadly spiritual chill fills the air.

The apostle Paul told the church at Ephesus: "Do not get drunk on wine, which leads to debauchery. Instead, be filled with the Spirit" (Eph. 5:18). If all Christians were already filled with the Spirit at all times, why would there be this strong command from Paul? Just a few verses before this Paul said, "Be very careful, then, how you live — not as unwise but as wise, making the most of every oppor-

If we're not Spirit-controlled, we will miss out on being what God wants us to be.

tunity, because the days are evil. Therefore do not be foolish, but understand what the Lord's will is" (vv. 15 – 17). It seems that Paul was saying we need to keep on being controlled by the Spirit if we want to live wisely, to understand the Lord's will for our lives, and to make the most of every opportunity. If we're not Spirit-controlled, we will miss out on being what God wants us to be.

So here's the question: If the Bible makes it clear that being controlled by the Spirit is so vital, what prevents so many of us from fully surrendering ourselves to the Holy Spirit?

Losing Control and Gaining Power

Some of us are afraid of opening up to the Holy Spirit because we prefer to stay in control. That's understandable. We're concerned about self-preservation, so giving up control can be scary. We're not sure we're comfortable with what God did in Acts 2 when people spoke in languages they had never learned. At the time, the early Christians' manifestations of euphoric joy and ecstatic utterances made people mockingly say, "Those people are drunk!" And we see their point. Why would God inspire such a holy bedlam?

Many of us want more of God but not to the point of being ridiculed. Our Western minds think, *I will serve the Lord, but I will remain in control as I do it.* But whether we like it or not, that's not how the church began. The church began with Spirit-controlled Christians who yielded themselves to God. That's radical, yes, but that's the way the Lord did it.

Some might say, "Yeah, but we've improved upon that New Testament style of Christianity." If that's true, I want to see the spiritual fruit our improvements have produced. People may have mocked those first, "unsophisticated" Christians, but thousands got saved in the first four chapters of Acts. The Word of God was treasured. The churches were filled with sacrificial love. A holy excitement pervaded the atmosphere. Have we really improved upon that?

In Acts 2, while the disciples gathered in one place, the Holy Spirit came upon them, and they spoke in languages they didn't know. I don't want to debate speaking in tongues, but I want to point out that when the Spirit came upon them, they immediately began to do something they couldn't do naturally. "When they heard this sound, a crowd came together in bewilderment, because each one heard their own language being spoken. Utterly amazed, they asked: 'Aren't all these who are speaking Galileans? Then how is it that each of us hears them in our native language?'" (Acts 2:6 – 8). They were speaking in actual languages they didn't know. They were doing something that could have no other explanation than that God was the source. The circumstances will differ from person to person, but an undeniable expression of Spirit-controlled living is that we will be lifted above the limitations of mere natural talents and abilities.

The irony of Spirit-filled living is that we have to give up power in order to gain a greater power. How many times in your Christian walk have you come to a place where you struggled to do something, so you just tried harder? Have you ever tried harder to have the self-discipline to read your Bible more or pray longer? Have you ever tried harder to love an unlovely person? Have you ever tried harder to be bold when you felt afraid? How did that work out for you? Trying harder has never gone well for me.

Christianity is not a self-effort religion but rather one of power — the ability and might of the Spirit. "For it is God who works in you to will and to act in order to fulfill his good purpose" (Phil. 2:13). The Spirit is the only one who can produce self-discipline, love, and boldness. But to do so, he has to control us daily. We can't rest on a religious experience we had years or even months ago.

Keep the Fire Going

Paul's last letter was written to Timothy, a young minister he had ordained. In the letter, Paul said: "For this reason I remind you to fan into flame the gift of God, which is in you through the laying on of my hands. For the Spirit God gave us does not make us timid, but gives us power, love and self-discipline" (2 Tim. 1:6–7). We get a picture of a fire that's almost out, embers that need to be breathed on to keep the fire alive. Paul wanted Timothy to fan the flames of the Spirit. He warned Timothy not to neglect them, but to stir up the fire and keep it going. Whatever Timothy did, he was to prevent the fire from being extinguished; he was to give attention to the Spirit's work in him. Without that anointing, Timothy would never fulfill the purposes of God for his life.

Charles Finney, a nineteenth-century Presbyterian minister and former president of Oberlin College, preached a series of lectures on revivals of religion, which later became a book and is now considered a spiritual classic. In it he describes three key points about the Holy Spirit:

- Jesus *promised* the Spirit's fullness. "You will receive power when the Holy Spirit comes on you; and you will be my witnesses in Jerusalem, and in all Judea and Samaria, and to the ends of the earth" (Acts 1:8).

- Scripture *commands* Christians to be filled with the Holy Spirit. "Do not get drunk on wine, which leads to debauchery. Instead, *be filled with the Spirit*" (Eph. 5:18, emphasis added). Just as there are commands to love one another and not to steal, "be filled with the Spirit" is no different. It is expressed in the imperative form, meaning it is a command no different from any other biblical command.
- The fullness of the Spirit is a *necessity* in our lives. When Jesus declared, "Apart from me you can do nothing" (John 15:5), he meant what he said.[2]

When God takes control of a life or a church, he takes control through the Holy Spirit, because the Holy Spirit is the Helper Jesus sent to do the job. When we fear giving control to the Spirit, we really fear God's control over our lives. When we refuse to yield to the Spirit, we miss out on the holy excitement of living beyond ourselves.

When we refuse to yield to the Spirit, we miss out on the holy excitement of living beyond ourselves.

As Paul told Timothy, God did not give him the spirit of timidity; rather, he gave power, love, and self-discipline. Notice, God is the one who gives those gifts, and it is only through the Holy Spirit working in our hearts that we receive them. We cannot live the life God desires for us without the presence of the Holy Spirit, but with him in control of our lives, our hope is in his power and his gifts are available for us to receive.

Would you like to love more deeply and more freely? Do you wish to have more self-discipline? Are your life and ministry producing fruit? For those things to happen, you have to surrender to the Helper. But oh the rewards that come when you hand control of your life to the Holy Spirit.

The Spirit waits to fulfill the mission he was sent to do — to govern the affairs of every born-again believer. I encourage you to get alone with God today and spend some time praying about who or what is in control of your life. You and I are going to be controlled by something. There is no question about that. So before you go any further, decide now whom you will yield to. Tell God your questions about being controlled by the Spirit. Present him with your hopes and longings for something more.

The first step in the process is giving him control.

Chapter 5

INFLUENCED AND CONTROLLED: ROMA'S STORY

Roma Black is a man in our church who used to be a successful player in New York City's drug and gambling scenes. He grew up under the influence of the street, and when he was old enough to make his own decisions, he gave control of his life to the evil that surrounded him.

But Roma had a praying mother, and God pursued him through every hellhole he ended up in. Christians also came into his life and showed him a love he had never experienced. Finally, Roma had to make a dramatic choice. Would he surrender to the Spirit's call, or would he let evil ultimately destroy him? I'll let him tell you in his own words.

ROMA

I grew up under the influence of gangsters and drug dealers in the drug-infested streets of Harlem in the 1960s and '70s. I was the seventh of nine kids born to a single mother; I never knew my father. Most mornings we stepped around dope addicts passed out in the stairwells of our tenement as we left for school. We bet money on whether or not they'd fall over while we watched. Sometimes I pushed 'em so I'd win the bet. Walking outside, it wasn't unusual to see a dead body in the backyard where somebody got their brains blown out and they froze during the night. There was a war going on in the streets, and death wasn't hidden from kids who lived there.

Although young, we saw what was going down around us. Guys would be outside shooting dice, and if the loser was short on money, the winner might pull out a pistol and shoot him. The shooter would walk away just like he came in. No emotion. Life meant nothing. We watched the blood bubbling out of the victim's head. We were so used to death that we'd stand there and count how many breaths the dying man took until he died. Then we'd scatter before the police got there.

You never wanted to be a witness. In Harlem, if you snitched, you died. If someone wanted you killed, all they had to do was put out a rumor that you were a snitch. That's all it took. Then you'd get killed. That's how dangerous it was during those times.

In the streets, you grew up fast. I started running numbers when I was ten. The number runners (those who ran illegal lotteries out of their businesses) would give me a bag of money and then give my description to a cop. I'd take the money and go play in the street until the cop pulled up and I heard, "Yo! Come here!" Then I'd take the bag over to his car, lean in, and drop the bag on the floor. I knew better than to hand it to the cop directly. The cop would then say something like, "Be a good boy, now. Go to school. And remember, respect police officers." I earned ten dollars for my efforts. But how could I respect someone who took bribes? Even as a young boy, I knew policemen who were on the take, crooked politicians, and immoral preachers. So I obviously didn't grow up respecting a whole lot of people in authority.

Kids in the suburbs, in affluent areas, wanted to become doctors or lawyers because those careers were respected and they made money. But growing up in the ghetto, the only career I wanted was to be a gangster. Gangsters and hustlers were my heroes. I looked up to them and respected them. They represented wealth, charisma, power, and prestige. We watched them ride down the street in fancy cars with beautiful women. We saw how they could take care of authorities by paying them off. So that's who I wanted to be like. When we played, we imitated those gangsters, mimicking their walk, talk, and swagger.

I didn't like school. I played hooky a lot, but even when I was there, I messed around. When I got in trouble, my mother would come to school and beat me. Back then it wasn't called abuse; it was discipline. She showed up at my classroom, and I'd assume the position — bent over a desk — and wait for the pain.

The first time I ever saw her cry was after I played hooky from school in the seventh or eighth grade. Instead of going to school, I'd spent the day with a friend robbing seven cab drivers. The old people in the neighborhood saw us. When we went after our last cab driver, they grabbed us and took us to the precinct and ratted us out. At the precinct, I still had all of the money shoved in my pockets. I asked an officer if I could use the bathroom, and once in there, I stashed the money behind the toilet so I could get it later. But when I went back, it was gone.

All of the cab drivers were at the precinct, and they were mad. I overheard them telling the officer, "We're going to press charges on this kid!"

That night at home my brothers and sisters heard what happened, and they taunted me.

"You're finally going away!"

"When he's gone, I get the top bunk!"

"They gonna put you in reform school!"

I went into my mother's room to see her, but when I walked in, she was on her knees praying and crying. As I watched, she fell prostrate on the floor, but she kept praying through her sobs. I ain't never seen her like that, and I slowly and quietly backed out of the room.

I was nervous on the day of the hearing. As I waited in the courtroom, I knew my future was about to change forever. But the cab drivers never showed up. Not one of the seven! All I could think was, *My mother's prayer saved me.*

The judge, however, was mad. "Where are these people? We're going to postpone this and do it again."

He set up another date. Again I sat nervously waiting for the proceedings to start, but once more, none of the cab drivers showed up! Although I'd been caught red-handed, the court couldn't do anything without witnesses, and I was allowed to go home.

Though we never talked about it at the time, I *knew* I was free because of my mother's prayers. Until then, my only experience with God had been going to church on Sunday and getting smacked upside my head when my brother and I talked during the service.

But I wasn't ready to give my life to anything but the streets. By the time I was fourteen, I was selling drugs. I had my own crew, and we sold around the block from my junior high school. Little bags of heroin sold for two dollars; fifteen bags were bundled and sold for thirty dollars, which was a lot of money at the time. I'd have two of the largest shopping bags you can imagine filled to the brim with bundles. I'd sit on the stoop and hold them for the dealers who'd collect the money and flash me a signal as to how many bundles to give the buyer. That way, if the dealer was caught, he didn't have any drugs on him. In those days, they didn't send kids to jail for dealing; the most we got was a warning or reform school.

My family moved to 118th Street between Fifth and Madison in Harlem, and I sold drugs a block away on 117th. They called it Junkie's Paradise. If you came around the block, you'd think you had stumbled upon a parade, because from one end of the street to the other, people were lined up to buy drugs. Dealers littered the entire street. I'd sell two shopping bags full of bundles in less than an hour while sitting on the stoop talking to girls. Friends who worked for me would be lookouts, making sure no one came out of the building behind me to take anything. We had lookouts everywhere.

Movies were an escape for me — an escape from the violence of the streets. I often sat in the theater for hours, longing for a different life than the one I lived. Sometimes I even cried. I knew something was wrong with me — tough guys didn't cry. But movies reminded me that I was human, that I could feel emotion, and that another life was out there somewhere waiting for me.

I continued to skip classes because I hated school, and finally in the tenth grade, I dropped out for good. One night after I had dropped out, we all went back to the junior high school; they used to let us play basketball there at night. After the game, we were hanging out with the gangsters, and one of them saw a junkie who owed them money. Big Zig, being an enforcer, grabbed the junkie and threw him against a wall. "Where's our money?"

The cab drivers never showed up.... All I could think was, *My mother's prayer saved me.*

"I don't have it," the guy said.

So Big Zig took an iron pipe — solid iron — and hit the guy in the head. He fell to the ground. All these years later, I can still hear the sickening thud. When that pipe hit his head, it hurt something inside of me. It affected me so badly, I told the guys I was going home.

"No, let's go get high."

"Let's go to the movies."

But I said no and left immediately; I didn't want them to see me crying. I could be brutal and hurt people, but I also had something tender inside of me. When I started to feel something, I thought, *I must be a sissy. Why am I crying?* You can't show that kind of emotion on the street, so I tried to detach myself from feelings of compassion.

When I was sixteen or so, I graduated from selling drugs near my junior high to a new spot on 116th and Eighth Avenue, way over on the West Side. It was a very, very dangerous drug marketplace. During that time, I remember my mom saying, "Son, there's going to come a time when money won't help you. If you die in your sin, you're going to hell." But that didn't move me. She was old school.

But I did know I was in a dangerous place for dealing drugs, so I moved to Brooklyn to lay low for a while. I stayed with my sister, intending to get paid to babysit her kids while I got out of the street life. But instead of getting better, I got in deeper. My sister was in the numbers racket, so I got into it too. Her boyfriend controlled whole blocks in Brooklyn, collecting payoffs from the illegal activities that went down there. So he got me a store on one of those blocks. I'd sit in front of the store with a bottle of champagne and sniff cocaine in broad daylight while I ran numbers in the store. I'd get so high that I actually walked on top of other people's cars. I'd be so zooted off cocaine that I'd exude all of this confidence, and that attracted women. Oh man, I had a woman for every day.

But I was empty inside.

My partner was a cocaine dealer, but his father was a preacher. One day I was at my store and Rev. Smith came in. You could always tell it was him, because he wore a collar Monday through Sunday.

"Roma Black," he said, "God's called you to be a preacher."

I was stunned. I thought the man was crazy. "You know what?" I said. "I know a little bit about the Bible, and it says that there is no hope for the devil." I literally called myself the devil, because I was under his influence. I knew I was working for Satan. And I knew that if I died, I was going straight to hell. I knew it.

Rev. Smith wasn't deterred. He looked me right in the eye and said, "No, God is calling you to preach."

But he didn't know what kind of iniquity went on in my store — selling drugs, smoking cocaine cigarettes, selling stolen goods, all kinds of illegal activity. Everything went on in there. We had a million-dollar-a-year racket business. No mob. No Italian connections.

One day I was in the back of my store and a young lady came in. She had the face of an angel. She held up a tract and said, "The Lord told me to give you this." She handed it to me, saying, "Jesus loves you."

I took the tract from her, balled it up, and threw it at her, hitting her in the face. "Get out of my store. I don't need no God. I make my own money. Church is for wimps and cowards, and I don't need God."

A few days later, another young lady came in and said, "I want you to read this."

So I did the same thing to her. "Get outta my store!" I said and hit her in the face with her own tract.

But after that, I started to think about those two ladies. They fascinated me. They both reacted the same way when I took their tracts and hit them in the face — they both looked at me with love. I was from the street. I lived a violent life. I was used to an eye for an eye. But even when I disrespected and cursed them, they looked at me with love. I was intrigued by their response.

Rev. Smith would come back occasionally, and I got to the point where I liked to see him. I'd see him coming and yell at my crew to put the drugs away. They begged me not to talk long, but sometimes I'd stay in the store for hours talking to Rev. Smith. My crew would get mad at me, but what could they do? I was tough, and I'd beat them if they complained.

But then things got very dangerous. I was in the store one day when an old gangster came in to play the numbers. When I learned his name, I said, "Hey, I knew a guy in Harlem with that name. He's a hit man, a gangster."

"Yeah, he's my son," the old gangster said, and we started talking.

About a month later, a brand-new black Mercedes pulled up in front of my store, and who got out? His son. He came into the store, and we started talking. "I know your dad," I told him.

We kicked it around, and then he said, "Come outside." So we went out to sit in his Mercedes and sniff cocaine. Sitting there, I could see his gun tucked in the right side of his pants.

A few weeks later, I was at another store and the black Mercedes showed up there. I knew this gangster was a very dangerous guy. He was a freelance contract killer for gangsters and the mafia. All of a sudden, he was coming around a lot. I also heard that he was asking about me. I'd tell the guys at my store, "Don't tell anybody where I am at." I was getting worried.

But this guy kept showing up. Every week I'd sit in his car and we'd talk and sniff cocaine, but I knew that he was one dangerous cat. I knew what he did. One day he and his dad came into the club we had in the back of the store. I told the bartender to set them up. "Give them a bottle of champagne." They just sat there, and I got a chill. All night long, I felt them watching me. They weren't there to enjoy themselves; they were there to *case me.*

I snuck out of the club because I was afraid and I didn't know what they wanted from me. The whole walk home, all I could think was, *What is going on?* I felt fear. And I felt death. But it was still a mystery. I knew who they were, and I knew they were casing me. *Am I a target? Is he clocking me because somebody wants me dead?*

In the Bible, Job said, "Lord, what I feared the most has come upon me." A few days later, I had my own Job experience. The black Mercedes pulled up to the store, and the hit man called me outside. By now I was frustrated. So I said, "What do you want from me?"

As I was sitting in his car, he turned to me, making sure he revealed the gun in his waistband. "You got a lovely girlfriend. You got a nice, cute little baby girl. Real cute. How's your mama doing?"

My hand started shaking as I realized how much he knew about me. "I've seen your place over on Ocean Avenue. And your business. I'm impressed.

> Even when I disrespected and cursed those ladies, they looked at me with love. I was intrigued by their response.

You're doing what? About a million dollars a year? I'm surprised. No mob connection; it's all brother-owned. That's impressive."

He knew everything about me, because that's what hitters do. Contract killers, they clock you. As he told me all that he knew, my hand shook so hard I was afraid he'd notice. I tried to be cool and not let him see that he had me, so I put my hand underneath my thigh. But he knew.

"I kicked your name around in Harlem, and everybody said you're a stand-up guy. You know how to keep your mouth shut. So this is what we're going to do...."

Whatever came next was an order not a request. Talking about my family was a threat. He would kill them, take them out one by one, and then kill me. He knew where I lived; he knew where my mother lived; he knew everything. Whatever he said next, I'd have to do. I swallowed hard and tried not to let my fear show.

"We're going to create a hit team. Like Murder Incorporated back in the '30s," he said, referring to an organized crime group responsible for hundreds of mafia killings. "But we're going to be bigger than them. I want you to recruit young men, and we're going to train them to be contract killers. You're going to be my man in Brooklyn. I got a guy for Harlem. I got a guy for the Bronx. We're going to make millions."

When he said that, everything flashed in front of me. Rev. Smith saying, "You're going to be a preacher." Those young girls giving me tracts. People walking down the street saying, "God's calling you."

There was no way out.... In my heart, I prayed to God, *If you're real, I need you now.*

But there was no way out. I was mean, violent, brutal, whatever words you wanted to use, but I had never killed anybody. Now that he'd told me his plan, I didn't have a choice; I had to become a hit man.

In my heart, I prayed to God, *If you're real, I need you now.*

As soon as I said it, the presence of the Lord came into the car. I felt it. It was like some incredible presence filled up the Mercedes. The hair on my neck stood up. My fear instantly vanished, and I suddenly felt bold. I turned to the hit man and pointed my finger at him and said, "I don't want no part of you or your plan. Besides, I am giving my life to Jesus Christ."

And when I said that, the entire atmosphere in the car changed. Suddenly this big thug became a little wimp, and in this strange, little-girl voice, he said, "Okay."

I opened the door to the car, and as I got out and walked back to my store, I braced myself because I knew he was going to shoot me. He had to. He'd just told me his plan in detail. But when I went into the store and turned to look out the door, the Mercedes was gone.

I've never seen him since.

I went inside and called my mother. "I had an experience with Jesus, and I don't know how to tell you about it, but I'm coming to church." I sat down in the store, and while everyone around me played numbers, I was lost in a zone. I remembered my mother's prayer, and tears rolled down my face. I wiped them away and said to myself, *God is real.*

But the devil wasn't done with me. He tried to pull me back in all kinds of ways. I tried to clean up my life on my own and failed. I prayed, *God, take away from my life anything that's sinful or anything that would lead me back to my old ways.*

God answered my prayer. All of a sudden, people would no longer deal with me. And my sisters with money — none of them would talk to me. Even Mom wouldn't talk to me when I called to tell her I was broke.

There was nothing I could do to save myself. The next Sunday I went to church. It was raining outside, but inside the place was on fire. I felt like the pastor was preaching my life. He called out sins of mine that only God and I knew I'd committed. Though I was sitting in the back and no one was around me, I felt like the pastor spoke right to me.

He made an altar call and asked those who wanted to accept Jesus as their Lord and Savior to come forward. There was movement at the front of the church as people accepted the pastor's invitation.

The last person came forward, and then there was an awkward pause. The pastor finally said, "I can't continue. I don't know what it is, but the Holy Spirit brought someone special here today. I don't know why, but he won't let me continue. This is your last chance." And then he made the invitation to receive Christ again.

With God as my witness, I lie not. I felt an invisible hand touch me on the shoulder. When that hand touched me, I felt such a spirit of love — an indescribable love. Tears rolled down my face, and I felt weak.

I couldn't fight it anymore. I got up and walked down the aisle, and when the pastor came over to me, I dropped to my knees. The pastor prayed over me, and I literally saw my life pass in front of my eyes — every dangerous scene, from that first day when I robbed those cab drivers, through every bad thing I did that could've cost me my life. With each scene that flashed through my mind, I heard a whisper:

"I saved you from that."

"I kept you from that."

"I watched over you there."

As the most recent scenes in my life played out, the store in Brooklyn, the gangsters I hung out with, and the conversations with the hit man, it felt like God was saying to me, "The very people you ran with wanted to kill you, and I saved you from that." I became aware that this was the day of salvation for me, and I better not miss it.

And as I prayed the sinner's prayer, I felt my sins being lifted. When I was able to open my eyes and look around, I saw my mother in the choir. She was sobbing, watching her black sheep give his life to Christ. Other people in the choir were fanning her to calm her down. She had been convinced that I was going to wind up in jail or the graveyard, but God flipped it. Isn't he amazing?

When I jumped up, I said to the pastor, "I feel so light!"

"Son, that's your sins. God has taken them and thrown them into the sea of forgetfulness, and he doesn't remember them anymore."

A month later, my girlfriend came to church to watch me get baptized. Ever since that day, I'd told everyone I knew that Jesus saves. Well, the day I got baptized, my girlfriend became a Christian too. We have been married for twenty-eight years, and Gladys has become an amazing prayer warrior.

A couple of years later, I went to visit Rev. Smith at his church. When I walked in wearing a suit and he looked up and saw me, he was stunned. He hadn't seen me for several years, and I'm sure he thought I was dead or in prison.

"Rev. Smith, you were right. I am saved, and I'm now serving the Lord."

It blew his mind.

Most of the people I grew up with are gone. They're dead. But I'm no longer serving Satan. I'm under the control of the Lord. He has used even what I experienced on the streets for his glory. Now when I am preaching in the streets and in prisons, I rely on his Spirit to guide me in what to say and when to say it. I'll preach wherever the Lord gives me an opportunity. When God saved me, he put me under new management.

I work for him now.

Part Two

WHEN GOD'S SPIRIT MOVES

Chapter 6

THE WORD COMES ALIVE

Alone in my London hotel room, I prayed that God would minister to me as I read the Bible. My heart was hungry. Far from home, I really felt my need for the Lord that day. I wanted to be fed in my innermost being. Although I knew I needed him every day, my spiritual hunger that morning was intense.

I read through the first few chapters in 1 Thessalonians from Weymouth's translation of the New Testament. I'd studied those chapters many, many times before, yet suddenly, powerful truth I'd never seen jumped off the pages at me. In those chapters, the apostle Paul revealed his ministerial heart in a unique way, and while meditating on it, my spiritual eyes were opened. For the first time, I became aware of something vital that was missing from my ministry, something that was probably missing from a lot of churches too. I sat on the floor and prayed, eventually falling prostrate as I wept. I saw where I had failed God. That day God spoke to me through his Word in a way that would help me for the rest of my life.

Not only did that revelation change my ministry forever, but I believe it has helped thousands of other leaders too. From that morning, I developed several messages I've preached to pastors around the world. Repeatedly, pastors have come up to me when I have preached it and said, "I needed to hear that. It was as if a light went on for me while you spoke."

I knew what they meant, because I felt as if a light had gone on that day in London for me too. But that wasn't an isolated occurrence. Spiritual illumination often occurs when I'm reading the Bible, and I know it does for many other believers too. Scriptures that were memorized as a child suddenly are understood with greater depth; a beloved Bible story is suddenly infused with rich layers of meaning.

How does that happen?

It's the teaching ministry of the Holy Spirit.

A Holy Appetite

As we already know, the Christian church was born when the Holy Spirit was poured out. Amazingly, in the hours afterward, thousands of people converted to the faith, and the new believers fell into an inspired new rhythm of congregational life. "They devoted themselves to the apostles' teaching and to fellowship, to the breaking of bread and to prayer" (Acts 2:42).

In the beginning, Christian doctrine was transmitted orally since there wasn't a written New Testament. The apostles spoke the gospel and the associated teachings they heard from Jesus. This was the Word of God that the early believers "devoted themselves" to. Other translations render the Greek in this passage as "they went on to give constant attention to" or "they occupied themselves continually."[1]

That kind of dedication to the Word is always a vital sign that the Holy Spirit is moving in the life of a person or a church. Believers have a hunger to hear, read, study, and in particular, understand more about the Word of God.

That makes sense, of course, since the Holy Spirit was the one who inspired the Bible. He was the author who inspired the writers. The Bible is his book. Spirit-controlled Christians don't usually have to force themselves to read the Bible; the Spirit gives them a holy appetite for it.

The Holy Spirit is the Spirit of truth, so he will always direct us toward God's truth. When a person has little interest in the Word, or when Scripture seems dull and tedious to a church body, that is a sign that something is seriously out of sync. When we don't have respect for the Word and reverence for its authority, and when we don't humble ourselves to hear what God has said, we're on the wrong path. And that's true regardless of whether it's done in the name of using cutting-edge technology, being relevant to today's culture, or relating to people at all costs.

I know that it's possible today to gather large numbers of people together on a Sunday without a strong emphasis on the Word. In fact, many of the people sitting in the pew might be totally content without hearing careful Bible preaching and exposition. But when we wander away from the Word, thinking we can live without it hour after hour, day after day, week after week, we cease to grow spiritually and open ourselves to spiritual deception. The apostle Peter wrote, "Like newborn babies, crave pure spiritual milk, so that *by it you may grow up* in your salvation" (1 Peter 2:2, emphasis added). The Word of God contains the vital spiritual nutrients we need — every day — to grow in Christ. Our cravings for more of God's Word aren't hunger pangs we work up. A holy appetite grows inside of us through the work of the Holy Spirit that causes us to crave truth.

> Is it possible that the Holy Spirit is a better teacher than even Jesus? Yes, because only he can teach us from the inside out.

A Divine Teacher for a Divine Book

Who better to teach us about God's Word than the person who wrote the book? But is it possible that the Holy Spirit is a better teacher than even Jesus? The short answer is yes, because only he can teach us from the inside out.

A BETTER TEACHER THAN JESUS?

I took geometry during my sophomore year in high school, and for the life of me, no matter what that teacher said, I couldn't figure it out. I didn't know an isosceles triangle from a bagel with cream cheese. None of it made sense. Then about two months into the semester, the teacher got sick and a new teacher replaced him. Under her tutelage, suddenly, the light went on for me. For the first time, I understood triangles, angles, and parabolas. (Well, maybe not the parabolas.) I had to give credit for my newfound understanding to the new teacher. It was the way she explained things that helped me understand geometry.

Many times I read the Bible, and I get stuck. I can read the sentence before me — the subject, the verb, the object — but I don't see the spiritual meaning for my life, nor does it find a place in my inner person. It's just a mental exercise. Does that ever happen to you?

Two thousand years ago, the disciples had Jesus as their teacher, though they called him by the more commonly used term of the time, rabbi. But even they had problems understanding what Jesus taught them. There are countless examples of Jesus saying something and the disciples completely missing the point. They just didn't get it. In fact, one of them even argued with him, saying, "No, you won't go to the cross. I won't let that happen." Jesus would teach them about trusting God, and in the next chapter, we see them not trusting God. Jesus even used himself as an example during a lesson about humility. During the Last Supper, Jesus showed himself as a servant of the Lord and washed the disciples' feet. Yet during that same dinner, the disciples argued about which one of them was the greatest (Luke 22:24 – 27).

But Jesus promised that when he died, another teacher would come and help them to properly digest spiritual truth. "I have much more to say to you, more than you can now bear. But when he, the Spirit of truth, comes, *he will guide you into all the truth*. He will not speak on his own; he will speak only what he hears, and he will tell you what is yet to come. He will glorify me because it is from me that he will receive what he will make known to you" (John 16:12 – 14, emphasis added).

Jesus not only told them a better teacher was on the way, but he also said the new teacher would convey truth that he couldn't pass on at that time. In other words, Jesus was saying, "I have more to say, and the new teacher will be the one to teach you about it." The Spirit "will guide you into all the truth," which includes applying the message to the hearts of the disciples. Then the meaning of Jesus' life and death, faith, hope, love, the power of prayer, and much more would all be made crystal clear to them.

TEACHING FROM THE INSIDE OUT

Just like any minister today, Jesus preached using only his voice. And just like any congregation today hearing a sermon, the disciples could hear his words only with their ears and process them with their minds. But the truth of God is different than mathematics or the laws of science. It can be understood and appropriated into our lives only when it is revealed to our innermost being; that is where its life-changing power works (Matt. 13:18 – 23).

A divine book must have a divine teacher so that its message can be revealed on a spiritual level. Otherwise the message just crumbles into facts that reside only in our brain cells. That Jesus was born in Bethlehem is a fact. Understanding the glorious meaning of Immanuel, God with us, and the significance of him lying in a stable requires divine teaching. So it is absolutely necessary for the Holy Spirit to be our teacher if the Bible is to be truly understood. The Spirit can overcome the human limitations of voice, ear, and brain. He teaches in the classroom of the heart.

Even when teachers do their best, the only way for us to be ultimately blessed by the Word is through the inner teaching of the Holy Spirit.

That is why we can read a portion of Scripture for years and then read it again, and *whammo*, it comes alive! We understand it in a brand-new way. We ask, *Why didn't I see that before?* That is the teaching ministry of the Holy Spirit.

Holy Spirit teaching is so important because Satan uses all kinds of things to deceive and lead believers and churches away from the truth. He can even use people who claim they are teaching the truth. For example, in 1 John we read a warning: "I am writing these things to you about those who are trying to lead you astray. As for you, *the anointing you received* from him remains in you, and you do not need anyone to teach you" (2:26 – 27, emphasis added).

Why would God say we don't need anyone to teach us when he was the one who put teachers into the church body?

Of course teachers play an important role, as do apostles, evangelists, prophets, and pastors. But even when teachers do their best, the only way for us to be ultimately blessed by the Word is through the inner teaching of the Holy Spirit. The Spirit is faithful to help us know truth from error and keep us from satanic distortions. But for all of that to happen, we must come with humble, teachable hearts.

The Eyes of the Heart

It is possible to find a simple believer just a few years in the Lord, in the mountains of Peru, who understands more about the Bible than a theologian with a PhD. In fact, that uneducated Peruvian may not just know more about the Bible, but he may also know the Lord in a way that the Greek or Hebrew scholar doesn't. Remember, it was Jesus who rejoiced and said, "I praise you, Father, Lord of heaven and earth, because you have hidden these things from the wise and learned, and *revealed* them to little children" (Luke 10:21, emphasis added).

It is easy for many of us to approach the Word of God daily with little dependence on the Holy Spirit. Often, we don't pray before we read the Bible even though we need his help to understand God's Word. The smarter and more educated we are, the harder it is for us to come like children, trusting the Spirit to make the Word real. But we also need to pray for pastors to preach with the help of the Spirit and for God to give us listening hearts so that the Word will build us up. We *must* have the Spirit's help, and if we ask in faith, he will help us.

The psalmist prayed, "Open my eyes that I may see wonderful things in your law" (Psalm 119:18). Notice that the prayer doesn't ask for open eyes to "read your law" or even to "understand your law." No, the psalmist's prayer asks God for something we rarely think about when we open the Word. "Open my eyes that I may *see* wonderful things *in* your law." He wasn't talking about his physical eyes. He was talking about the eyes of his heart.

We all have two sets of eyes. We have the eyes in our head, and we have the eyes of the heart, which the Bible refers to in many places (e.g., Eph. 1:18). The process of seeing spiritual things through the eyes of the heart, not merely the mind, is called "revelation." It's not some wild and woolly, holy-roller craziness. It's an everyday working of the Holy Spirit in all who desire it.

In that same psalm, the writer also says: "Praise be to you, LORD; *teach me* your decrees" (Ps. 119:12, emphasis added). He isn't content just to read them. No, he calls out to God, "Lord, you gave me your words, but now you must come and make them clear." He recognizes that he can't do it on his own.

Too many of us pick up the Bible and read it like we are reading the *New York Times* or *People* magazine. We're confident in our ability to understand Scripture because we might have a high IQ or because we went to school and got a degree from a university. But we'll only understand the shell of it that way. Sure we'll gain some facts; we might even understand some sketchy truths; but spiritual teaching that transforms our lives will elude us.

In a later chapter, we'll look at D. L. Moody, who was one of the greatest evangelists of all time. Yet he didn't have a high IQ and he wasn't educated in a seminary. In fact, he was semiliterate! How did he become such an effective preacher, drawing huge crowds and leading thousands of people to Jesus without an education? He was taught by the Holy Spirit.

As a speaker, I have found that organizing material into a three-point message with a conclusion is not the hard part. Rather, the hard part is allowing the Spirit to make the passage real to my heart. If I am going to preach about love, for example, and the Holy Spirit hasn't dealt in a fresh way with me about the unfathomable depth of God's love and my sad lack of it, how will I effectively stir my listeners with God's truth?

Preaching becomes most effective when God has granted the speaker spiritual revelation through the Spirit. Without his assistance, we pastors can easily preach in a self-righteous, judgmental manner because we haven't confronted our own shortcomings and our need for God's grace. We will fail to have compassion for the congregation. I'll admit, I've preached those kinds of sermons. May they be obliterated forever! But when the Spirit has opened both the Word and the speaker's heart, the message will edify and encourage.

Pride and Prejudice

If we repeatedly read the Bible without the help of the Holy Spirit, it tends to reinforce our own prejudices and rock-hard doctrinal positions. We end up merely finding ammunition for what we already believe. We become so spiritually proud, so convinced of our own positions, that the Spirit is hindered in helping us to grow in the things of God.

Go back to the 1850s in America when that horrible institution of slavery was being challenged and abolitionists raised their voices against slaveholders. In the South, there were Bible-thumping preachers who twisted God's Holy Word to defend the wickedness of slavery. Some actually held that the enslavement of African-Americans was part of God's purpose for the earth! With closed minds and bitter hearts, they used the Word of God for unholy purposes. And their congregations shouted, "Amen!" Those bigots weren't ungodly atheists; they were ministers and congregants with open Bibles before them. Talk about spiritual deception!

The same thing had happened to the religious leaders of Jesus' day. They held a prejudiced view of what the Messiah would be like and what he would do when he came. Remember when Nathanael said, "Can anything good come out of Nazareth?" At the time, Jerusalem was divided into two providences. The south was considered to be more devout while the north was considered to be more secular because of the influence of the trade routes. Jesus came from Galilee in the northern providence, and so the religious leaders were all thinking the same thing as Nathanael. How could the Messiah come from there? Jesus didn't fit into their theology because their hard hearts were darkened — even as they taught from the Scripture.

But Jesus said to them, "*You study the Scriptures* diligently because you think that in them you have eternal life. These are the very Scriptures that testify about me, yet you refuse to come to me to have life" (John 5:39 – 40, emphasis added). The fact was they were too blind to see that the Messiah the Scriptures promised was standing five feet in front of them!

When we see only what we want to see in the Bible, it loses all power to transform us.

The leaders who plotted Jesus' death were the religious fundamentalists of their day. Not only did they hold the Law in great reverence; they worshiped it. But did they understand its true meaning? No. They referenced God's Word without any spirit of revelation, brokenness, or submission to God. Without the help of the Holy Spirit to understand the meaning of what we read, we're susceptible to reading our own biases into God's Holy Word. No wonder our reading can become dry and boring. When we see only what we want to see in the Bible, it loses all power to transform us.

Rocking the Boat of Our Traditions

I find that most believers don't change more than 5 percent from what they believed when they were only two years in the Lord. Imagine any other field of study where people didn't progress in their knowledge and understanding of the subject. If a student in the eleventh grade were still operating with his second-grade education, we would say something had gone tragically wrong with his education.

Yet, because we grow up in a certain tradition, we develop a narrow sectarian view of truth. When confronted with Bible verses and truth uncomfortable to us, we hide behind, "But this is the way we've always done it. This is what we've always believed." I've heard folks say, "This is our Baptist way of doing things." Or the Presbyterian way, or Pentecostal way, or Lutheran way, or Catholic way. Substitute your own denomination or church name. After two years in that climate, anything in the Bible that rocks their boat and challenges their assumptions is dismissed with: "It can't mean that. It must have another meaning in the Greek."

When we pick up the Bible and don't ask for the Spirit's help, it's like saying, "God, do a new thing in me, but I'm not going to change anything I believe." That's an odd prayer, isn't it? No wonder we grow so little in our faith and see so few converted to Christ. William Law, an eighteenth-century English devotional writer, said, "Thousands stand ready to split doctrinal hairs and instruct others in the fine meaning of Scripture words — but there are so few through whom the Holy Spirit can work to bring [people] to new birth in the kingdom of God."[2]

Often we get our definitions for important things not by what the Spirit shows us in Scripture, but by what we saw growing up in church. "Oh, that's what preaching is!" Or, "That's what worship should look like, because that's the way we've always done it in the church I attend." It is difficult for all of us to come to the Word of God and say, "Holy Spirit, teach me, even if it goes against what I've been conditioned to believe." And yet we must. We will never understand God's purpose for the church and us individually unless we humble ourselves and pray, "Spirit of the living God, fall fresh on me!"

Every January, many of us make New Year's resolutions to read our Bibles more. But without the Spirit's help, our carnal human tendencies often overcome that resolution. And when we do open the Word, we often read matter matter-of-factly, just to say we have had our "devotional time." I can tell you from my own experience, devotional times that are rushed or mechanical lead to days that don't go very well.

It takes time for the Holy Spirit to teach us in our hearts the meaning of a passage. If we don't wait on the Holy Spirit, trusting him, we can grow cold and fall out of communion with God even while having devotions every day. We'll just be heaping up verses, maybe even memorizing them; we'll know the references, but we'll miss the wonderful teaching of the one who was promised to guide us into all truth. But when we allow the Spirit to teach us, oh the understanding, the joy, and the insight that comes from the Word.

The apostle Paul wrote, "'What no eye has seen, what no ear has heard, and what no human mind has conceived' — the things God has prepared for those who love him — *these are the things God has revealed to us by his Spirit*. The Spirit searches all things, even the deep things of God" (1 Cor. 2:9 – 10, emphasis added).

If you and I want to grow in our spiritual lives, we can. As we open our hearts to the Holy Spirit working with the Word, we can even understand the deep things of God. Don't you long for that?

That's what I want.

Every time we open the Bible, let's stop and pray, whether for fifteen seconds or for fifteen minutes, asking the Spirit to teach us. When I read the Bible, I want God to talk to my soul. "Teach me knowledge and good judgment, for I trust your commands" (Psalm 119:66). Then our lives will be more like Jesus every day.

Chapter 7

THERE ARE SIGNS AND SYMBOLS OF RENEWAL

After a recent Tuesday night prayer meeting, I was introduced to a pastor who was visiting with a small group of leaders from his church. I welcomed him and asked where he was from.

"Kentucky," he answered.

"That's quite a ways from New York City," I replied. "How long will you be here?"

"We're heading back home tonight. I left at dawn this morning just to be in the prayer meeting."

I was shocked. "Really? All that way for just one service?"

"Brother, I'm thirsty for God," he said with all seriousness. "I can't go on anymore. I'm worn out and burned out. I'm desperate for something fresh from God's Spirit."

As the pastor spoke, I couldn't help but think of David's plea at the beginning of Psalm 63:

> You, God, are my God,
>   earnestly I seek you;
> I thirst for you,
>   my whole being longs for you,
> in a dry and parched land
>   where there is no water.
>
> *verses 1 – 2*

65

Have you ever felt dried out and run down in your Christian life? When that happens, a lot of us just keep plugging away until the point of spiritual exhaustion. Some folks give up and play the hypocrite, pretending to be someone they aren't. The old saying "If you run around, you run down, and then you want to run away" is true. But there is a remedy to those dry periods when we have run around too much, and it's found in what the apostle Peter called "times of refreshing" from the presence of the Lord (Acts 3:19).

Symbols for Life

The Bible uses a number of symbols to make the work of the Holy Spirit understandable to us. Later we'll talk about wind, a dove, and oil. After that we'll spend some time talking about fire. But when we talk about being refreshed by the Holy Spirit, the symbol that best helps us understand how that can happen is water.

WATER

In the Old Testament, where there was no water, there was no life. People died during droughts. Likewise, unless the living water of the Spirit is flowing in us, we and our churches will have an absence of spiritual life and little vitality. Just as in the Mojave Desert, no water equals no life, no growth, and no fruit. We can attend church regularly and have perfect doctrine, but without the Holy Spirit to water us, we will wither and die.

Jesus talked openly about the life-giving properties of the Spirit. "On the last and greatest day of the festival, Jesus stood and said in a loud voice, 'Let anyone who is thirsty come to me and drink. Whoever believes in me, as Scripture has said, rivers of living water will flow from within them'" (John 7:37 – 39). By "rivers of living water," Jesus was referring to the Spirit that believers would later receive.

When the Spirit of God comes, we have new life. Without the Spirit of God, we're left to struggle with our self-effort, which is riddled by moral weakness and sinful tendencies. But when the Spirit comes, we have joy, hope, and power. Notice that Jesus doesn't refer to a drop of water but to "rivers of living water." Like a river, the Spirit flows — a force of power that comes into us and then flows out so we can be a blessing to others.

God uses water as a symbol of the Holy Spirit in a slightly different way when he says, "I will be like the dew to Israel; he will blossom like a lily" (Hos. 14:5). We all have witnessed the grass and flowers glistening with tiny drops of refreshing water. By using this metaphor, God is saying he will be like the dew, which settles quietly in the night and coats the ground by morning. Dew can't form when conditions are too hot or the wind is too strong. Likewise, we can't be refreshed by God when we're too busy running around.

I've had hard times in my life when I got dry and worn out and the Spirit ministered to me like dew. For me, dew comes when I am sitting in his presence. I've missed the Spirit more than once in my life because my busyness robbed me of the quiet refreshing times that come from the Lord.

> I've missed the Spirit more than once in my life because my busyness robbed me of the quiet refreshing times that come from the Lord.

Sometimes after our prayer meetings, people will sit quietly, or perhaps kneel and pray, lingering for a while longer. They don't want to get up and leave. They want to remain in the presence of God. They want to enjoy the dew of heaven as they wait before the Lord. That is one reason we don't schedule meetings too close together on Sunday. If people feel rushed, if leaders hint that they have to clear the sanctuary so the next meeting can start, sweet times of waiting in the Spirit's presence can easily be missed.

Even during the services, I try to be sensitive to the Spirit's voice. I sometimes need to pause and wait for some sense of what to do next. Visitors may wonder, *Why isn't anyone saying something? The meeting is sagging a bit. Come on, why don't they get going to the next thing on the agenda?* But God never meant for a church service to be a production. Instead, what's of paramount importance is that people experience the Lord and have an opportunity to be refreshed by the water of the Spirit.

On occasion we have prayer meetings that start at 9:00 on a Friday evening and continue past midnight. The last time we scheduled one, more than two thousand people came to worship, pray, and wait on the Lord. At times it was loud as we made a joyful noise to the Lord, but at other times we prayed quietly or waited silently.

Once, around 1:30 in the morning, I was sitting on the steps of the altar area. I looked up to see that there were still more than a thousand people in the sanctuary, waiting, praying, or quietly rejoicing. The presence of God was so real that I whispered, "Lord, I think I could stay right here for the rest of my life." The atmosphere seemed saturated with divine love and grace, and the thought of leaving it was unthinkable. The dew of God's Spirit had settled on us in a wonderful way.

WIND, A DOVE, AND OIL

The Bible has other symbols for the Holy Spirit besides water. One is wind, which in the original Greek in the New Testament is the same word as *breath*. Wind helps us to visualize the invisible and mysterious movement of the Spirit (John 3:8). A dove symbolized the Spirit during Jesus' baptism. "Just as Jesus was coming up out of the water, he saw heaven being torn open and the Spirit descending on him like a dove" (Mark 1:10). The Holy Spirit is all-powerful yet strangely gentle and sensitive in his dealing with us. We can all too easily grieve him.

Oil is a symbol often used for the Holy Spirit in the Old Testament. The anointing of the Holy Spirit is likened to the oil that was put on almost everything in the tabernacle. When it was built as a place of worship, not only were the temple objects anointed with oil, but so also were the priests. Later the elders of the early church were instructed to pray for the sick and to anoint ailing believers with oil as a symbol of the Spirit (James 5:14).

FIRE

Fire is one of my favorite symbols for the Holy Spirit. It is used to represent the power and presence of God. When John the Baptist came on the scene before Jesus appeared, he said, "I baptize you with water. But one who is more powerful than I will come.... He will baptize you with the Holy Spirit *and fire*" (Luke 3:16, emphasis added).

Jesus never baptized anyone with water. Why? Because the baptism he would administer was the baptism of the Holy Spirit and fire. Don't mistake those words as indicating two baptisms, one of the Spirit and another one of fire. Instead, Luke was using imagery — fire as a symbol representing the Spirit — to describe *one* baptism. Jesus baptizes in the consuming fire of the Holy Spirit.

Consuming Fire

If you light a match and set a piece of wood on fire, the fire will *penetrate* the wood. That's what the Holy Spirit does in our lives.

He goes beyond surface appearances to the root of our beings. The Spirit doesn't put Band-Aids on anything — he goes to the core of your problems to provide help. Likewise, preaching that is anointed by the Holy Spirit is fiery preaching. That doesn't mean beating people down or condemning them; rather, it means ministry that penetrates the heart, reveals sin, and vividly shows the need for Jesus Christ. Without the Holy Spirit's fire, preaching can descend to mere entertainment or displays of oratory.

> **The Spirit doesn't put Band-Aids on anything — he goes to the core of your problems to provide help.**

When Peter preached the first sermon of the Christian era, those ineloquent but fiery words produced deep conviction and a response of, "What shall we do?" (Acts 2:37). Teaching aids that help preachers communicate are useful, but without the Spirit's fire, hearts will never be humbled and broken before the Lord.

In Jeremiah, God asked, "Is not my word like *fire*?" (Jer. 23:29, emphasis added). The Word preached with the Spirit's fire cuts through the clutter and deals with the troubled condition of our hearts. Many people probably have little interest in experiencing God's fiery word; they prefer entertaining services and sermons that aren't confrontational. But the Spirit's fire always cuts to the chase and deals with the hindrances that keep us from the blessing of God.

The great temptation today in Christianity is to make our message so palatable to the masses that we lose the element of fire. We create services filled with candy and fluff. But that will not extend the kingdom and see Jesus glorified. People cannot come to God without the fiery work of the Holy Spirit.

I'll never forget one such personal experience with God years ago when I was new to the ministry. I was praying alone before a Tuesday evening service. At that time, the church was housed in a little rundown building, and I knew we would have fewer than ten people attending that night's prayer meeting. I had been praying that God would draw more people to the church and increase the enthusiasm of the congregation. As I prayed, the Spirit worked. He went right to my core and seemed to say, "The main problem is not the lack of people and their spiritual immaturity. You're the one who needs to be changed first. You're lacking in compassion for the people, and you do not love them the way I want you to. In your insecurity, you're just trying to get through another meeting."

Talk about fire! Talk about penetration! That wasn't easy to hear. I ended up on my face before God. I had come to ask God to help me with all of the people problems of the church, and instead his fire penetrated to *my problem*. When the Spirit works in our lives, he keeps us away from superficial excuses and the blame games we like to play. Fire burns away the false and leads us to the truth.

JUNK IN THE BONFIRE

In the second-floor lobby of our church, we have a large painting of an early 1900s Salvation Army street meeting in New York City. The war cry, or motto, of the Salvation Army was "Blood and fire." Blood represented the blood Jesus shed to save all people, and fire represented the Holy Spirit, who was sent to equip believers and transform lives. Catherine Booth, the wife of William Booth, the founder of the Salvation Army, understood the importance of fire as a symbol for the Holy Spirit. Known as the mother of the army, Catherine became very famous in her own right. I once read something she said that has stuck with me, although I must paraphrase it because I can't remember the actual source. Around 1890, she said, "I travel around the country, and I hear a lot of eloquent words and many sermon masterpieces. But what my soul longs for are burning words."

Catherine wanted anointed messages that penetrated, stirred, and produced brokenness of heart. She felt her need and knew that change happens from the inside out. She was a leader who taught God's Word and understood the difference between sermons that were just words and those that God had inspired to change lives.

The prophet Malachi wrote, "[God] will sit as a refiner and purifier of silver; he will purify the Levites and refine them like gold and silver" (Mal. 3:3). When the Holy Spirit searches our hearts, he is like a purifying fire. Just as a good fire burns out dross and impurities, unworthy things are burned out of our lives when we allow the Spirit to do his work.

When people are intent on getting rid of a lot of junk, they often simply start a bonfire and toss the things that they no longer want into the flames. Fire burns everything that is worthless. Sometimes we just need a good Holy Spirit fire to touch our lives. The pure, godly things will remain because they are like silver, gold, and precious stones. Fire won't destroy them; in fact, they will be purified. But the wood, hay, and junk in our lives and churches will be burned away.

CATCH THE FIRE!

When the Holy Spirit sets a person's life on fire, the Spirit doesn't stop there. The fire spreads, setting other people aflame too. I love that about the Holy Spirit. When someone is on fire with the love of God — they love the Word and love to pray — the next thing you know, people around them are inspired to do the same. There isn't anything forced or pushy about it. It just happens, because it is the nature of fire to spread.

A growing number of people are longing for the Holy Spirit's fire. They love their pastor, and they love their church. They are born-again Christians, yet they know something is missing. When they read their Bible, they feel it. Every year I get hundreds of email messages from people saying, "I need the fire." Of course, they don't always use the word *fire*, but that's what they mean. They're unsatisfied by their own spiritual lives. They also know God has much more planned for their churches. Some tell me they have every attraction a church could want: an activities center, a gym, great music, and sophisticated audiovisual elements. The pastor is a good man, yet people visit and few stay to grow in the Lord. And although the younger generation was raised by Christian parents, by the time they graduate from high school, they turn their backs on the things of God.

> **When someone is on fire with the love of God, . . . people around them are inspired to do the same.**

We can never do what the Spirit can do. No amount of human talent and exertion of energy will ever grow the spiritual kingdom of Christ. We need to return to depending on the Spirit's fire, which not only quickens and penetrates but also illuminates our path.

A LIGHT IN THE DARK

When I was ten, my family lived on Parkside Avenue in Brooklyn near Prospect Park. We lived in a small railroad apartment, so called because it had three narrow rooms in a straight line, like boxcars. My older brother, younger sister, and I shared the only real bedroom. My parents slept on a pullout sofa in the living room, no more than twenty feet away from us. We obviously were a very *close* family.

One night I got up in the middle of the night and went downstairs to the unfinished basement for some reason. It was cluttered with boxes, crates, and my dad's woodworking tools and supplies. I was too small to reach the light, so I walked through the basement in the dark. I wasn't worried because I knew every inch of that area. Or at least I thought I did until I rammed my bare foot into a heavy box.

"Owwww!" I screamed in excruciating pain. I sank down to the floor, crying and grabbing my foot in agony. I thought I would pass out from the pain. I sat in the dark until the pain subsided enough for me to hobble back upstairs.

Two days later, I was still sore. But I learned a lesson that we all learn one way or another: walking in the dark can be dangerous. If the lights had been on, I would have avoided all that pain. I would have seen the box and stepped around it.

For most of the world's history, fire, not electric light bulbs, has illuminated dark nights. Fire helped people see where they were going so they could avoid unseen dangers. It helped them to avoid running into things that blocked their paths or that were coming toward them in the dark.

Thank God that the Holy Spirit's fire also produces light — something we desperately need in a world full of difficult decisions and hidden dangers. The Spirit illuminates our lives and our choices so that we can see the path ahead and know what to avoid. Yet too often we don't seek the Holy Spirit's direction when it comes time to making vital decisions. Even religious organizations often rely only on human intelligence rather than the Holy Spirit's light for critical decision making. A preacher recently told me that he had attended a board meeting for a Christian ministry. He noticed that no one prayed before it started. There was also no prayer during the meeting, and when it came time to make a difficult decision, not one person suggested trying to find the mind of Christ. No one thought to pray, "Jesus, we don't know what to do. Send us your Spirit."

The Holy Spirit is God's only agent on earth. He was sent here to guide us. If you read the book of Acts, you'll see that a computer-mapping program didn't govern Paul's trips. The illumination of the Holy Spirit guided his path. In fact, the Spirit forbade Paul from going to some places — not because they didn't need to hear the gospel, but because God had another plan. And the apostle waited until the Spirit's direction could guide him into it.

STOKE THE FIRE

To the believers in Thessalonica, Paul wrote, "Do not put out the Spirit's fire" (1 Thess. 5:19).[1] Amazingly, although the Holy Spirit is fully God, it is entirely possible for believers like you and me to hinder his work and quench his sacred fire. Some people falsely believe that whatever God wants to do he will do. Consider Jesus' invitation to his own church in Laodicea: "Here I am! I stand at the door and knock. If anyone hears my voice and opens the door, I will come in and eat with that person, and they with me" (Rev. 3:20). If he's Christ, and he wants in, why doesn't he just come in? Why does he bother knocking and asking? That's the mystery of God's sovereignty and our free will. We must respond to him, or we will miss out on his planned blessing.

Earlier I wrote about Paul telling Timothy to stir up the embers, to keep the fire going. We need to do the same thing. For some of us, the embers are faintly glowing, and we need to tend to them, stir them up so they will burst into open flame.

Thank God for financial resources, equipment, talent, education, and new translations of the Bible. But for most of us, the greatest need is still more *fire*. We need the fire of the Holy Spirit changing our lives and our local assemblies. We need it spreading throughout our towns and cities, spreading so Christ can be glorified. May that be our prayer today. *Send the fire, God. Burn, penetrate, change, renovate, illuminate. Do as you promised, as we wait in Christ's name.*

Chapter 8

THERE IS JOY

In the late eighties, Bobby McFerrin wrote and performed a little song called "Don't Worry, Be Happy." The song had a Caribbean feel to it, but instead of using instruments to accompany his voice, McFerrin recorded it a cappella. All of the "music" came from over-dubbed vocals, whistling, and other sounds made by McFerrin. The song hit number one on the charts, and people enjoyed singing along with the happy little tune. Of course, the message offered a great psychological boost too. Don't worry. Just be happy. Let go of your anxieties and enjoy life. It made sense. Being happy is probably something we'd all like to do more. But that leads to a simple question: how?

Happiness versus Joy

Happiness ebbs and flows based on our changing circumstances. A new baby or grandchild is born, and we're all smiles. We win a free vacation, and we're ecstatic! The boss gives a big raise just when we need the extra money, and we're elated. But the euphoria is only temporary. Inevitably something changes and takes our happiness with it. The baby gets sick; our vacation gets rained on; our job is eliminated by a corporate merger. The positive feeling is fleeting. At best we're left feeling empty, and at worst, even angry.

So how do we get our happiness back when the situation changes?

We can't wish happiness back. We can't chase it. Trying harder to regain it only produces frustration. If circumstances alone make us happy, then our situation has to change for us to be happy again. Yet that's precisely the reason we're unhappy. We don't, and never will, have control over the things that make for "don't worry, be happy."

Happiness is circumstantial and elusive, but joy is not circumstantial. We can have joy even when we're not happy. Some may hear Christians talking about joy and think that *joy* is just a religious word for happiness. But joy differs from happiness. If the situation is right, anyone can experience happiness. Even people who don't know God or who curse God can be happy. But they don't have joy, for that blessing in life has a totally different source.

According to Scripture, the Holy Spirit produces joy. "But the fruit of the Spirit is love, *joy*, peace, forbearance, kindness, goodness, faithfulness, gentleness and self-control" (Gal. 5:22–23, emphasis added). Isn't it interesting that joy is mentioned immediately after love? Obviously God doesn't want us to live depressed, cranky, and bitter lives. He knows that happiness is fleeting, so through the Spirit, he gives us supernatural joy that transcends our circumstances. Joy is a beautiful gift that accompanies salvation through faith in Jesus Christ. It is a gift imparted by the Holy Spirit to our innermost being.

Inexpressible and Glorious Joy

If joy is a gift, we should expect to see more of it in the church, yet we're often surprised when we do. However, when we recognize that true joy doesn't come from our circumstances but rather from God, we begin to see joy as a blessing for everyday life. And that joy from the Spirit will make us distinctive to the culture around us.

HIV POSITIVE AND FULL OF JOY

A certain woman in our church is known for her sunny disposition and the joy in her heart; she's a real saint of God. One day more than fifteen years ago, she came to my office and said she needed to talk.

"I just found out that I have HIV," she said. "I contracted it from my husband. He's a drug addict."

I sat forward in my chair and lowered my head, thinking of the devastation in that sentence.

"I'm here for two reasons, Pastor. The first is that I wanted to tell you personally so you wouldn't hear it from someone else. The second is because I need counsel on whether I should tell my children, and if so, when would be the best time? I don't want them to be hurt if I don't tell them, but I don't want them to worry either."

As she told me this, she was amazingly composed. There was a sweetness about her spirit that caught me totally off guard. A part of me wanted to ask, "What planet do you come from?" But instead we talked, and then I prayed for her. When we finished, she asked sincerely, "Can I pray for you?"

That sweet lady started out by telling me she was HIV positive and then finished by praying for *me*! She hadn't read some book on positive thinking and then decided to give it a try. She hadn't psyched herself up to send good vibes into the universe so they would come back to her. This was a woman experiencing joy despite some very painful and underserved circumstances.

JOY MAKES US DISTINCTIVE

The kind of joy this woman had was normal for the New Testament church, and it should be normal for us too. Should we be depressed that Jesus died for our sins and rose from the grave and that all of our sins are forgiven? Should we lament the knowledge that one day we're going to be with the Lord forever? Should the fact that our name is written in the Book of Life make us sad? No. Those things should give us great joy.

Peter wrote: "Though you have not seen [Jesus], you love him; and even though you do not see him now, you believe in him and are

> **The kind of joy this woman had was normal for the New Testament church, and it should be normal for us too.**

filled with an inexpressible and *glorious joy*, for you are receiving the end result of your faith, the salvation of your souls" (1 Peter 1:8 – 9, emphasis added). Does an "inexpressible and glorious joy" describe your church or mine? It should. The epistle to Rome is Paul's great theological document regarding justification by faith and other weighty doctrinal matters. Yet toward the end of his letter, the apostle declares that the kingdom of God isn't essentially about doctrinal positions such as Calvinism or Arminianism. The kingdom isn't about who is right in the pretribulation or posttribulation rapture debate. Paul said that the kingdom of

God is a matter of "righteousness, peace and *joy* in the Holy Spirit" (Rom. 14:17, emphasis added). That is how important joy is; it makes us distinctive as followers of Jesus Christ.

I'm not talking about emotionalism, however, not worked up frenzies or singing choruses endlessly until we create a certain vibe. I don't want that, and neither do you. What the apostle Paul described was a life of joy that comes from the Spirit. He wrote to the Thessalonian believers, "You welcomed the message in the midst of severe suffering with the joy *given* by the Holy Spirit" (1 Thess. 1:6, emphasis added).

If we saw a church filled with prejudice and anger, we would say, "That can't be a Christian church." Why? Because God is love, and the fruit of the Spirit is love. If there is no love, if there is a nasty atmosphere, then it can't be of God and of the Spirit.

Why shouldn't we draw the same conclusion when we see a joyless church? We often rationalize about why our lives aren't joy-filled, but we don't find depressed, cranky believers in the New Testament.

In the little church I grew up in, there was a middle-aged woman who was always dressed in black. She wore a black dress, a black hat, and black shoes. She always sat alone with a tight, pursed look on her face, and she never talked to anyone. I never even saw her smile. She would enter into the meetings and pray and listen to the Word and then leave. As a young child, I was afraid to even get near her. She looked like she had been baptized in lemon juice!

One day I got up the courage to ask another adult about her. "What's with that lady?" I asked.

The man gave me an understanding nod as if he knew from experience something that I didn't. "Oh, her. You can tell she walks very close to God."

My little mind struggled with the thought. *Walking close to God means you never smile? It means you have no friends? You never rejoice in Jesus?* Why would anyone want to get close to God if that's what it did to you? Yet that is the picture some people have of God's plan for the Christian life — dark, somber, and joyless.

When we walk in the Spirit, when the Spirit controls us, he produces joy in our lives just as he produces love. Luke even described Jesus as "full of joy *through* the Holy Spirit" (Luke 10:21, emphasis added). All joy comes from the Holy Spirit. We can't manufacture it, call it up, try harder to get it, or make it happen on our own.

Nobody Knows the Trouble I've Seen

"Easy for you to say, Pastor Cymbala," some people might say. "You don't know what I've been through! If people had been as nasty to you as they were to me, you wouldn't think all this joy stuff is so easy."

Those people have no idea what scars I am walking around with, just as I have no idea of the hurts they have suffered. But joy isn't promised only to those with the least pain in their lives. Joy is for everyone willing to be controlled by the Spirit. Jesus said, "Blessed are you when people hate you, when they exclude you and insult you and reject your name as evil, because of the Son of Man. Rejoice in that day and leap for joy, because great is your reward in heaven" (Luke 6:22–23).

When life is painful, when people hate and act ugly, Jesus says that we don't have to lose our joy.

When life is painful, when people hate and act ugly, Jesus says that we don't have to lose our joy. To suggest that past suffering somehow gives us the right to be joyless is just one way to avoid the truth.

But even Jesus knew what sorrow was, and he knew what it was to weep. Isaiah prophesied that Jesus would be a man of sorrows (Isa. 53:3), and that prophecy certainly came true. He suffered both on the cross and off the cross as he was mocked, beaten, and humiliated. But if this is our image of Jesus — the mournful Son — we have only half the picture.

In Hebrews we learn that God anointed Jesus with the oil of joy (1:9). As we discussed in chapter 7, oil is a symbol of the Holy Spirit. And as we just read in Luke 10:21, Jesus was *full of joy* through the Holy Spirit. What a strange juxtaposition! Jesus was a man of sorrows who bore the cross, yet he was anointed with joy. And his joy, like ours, came from the Holy Spirit. To truly understand Jesus, we can't see him only as a mournful Savior. We have to balance that with the other truth — that he was filled with joy and spent much of his time rejoicing.

"Well sure," some might say, "he is Jesus! If he could be fully God and fully man at the same time, no wonder he could experience sorrow and joy. But I'm not Jesus." Fortunately, Jesus isn't the only example of simultaneous sorrow and joy that we're given. The apostle Paul said that he was at times "sorrowful, yet always rejoicing" (2 Cor. 6:10).

Is that possible?

No matter what the pain, pressure, or heartache we're going

through, it's possible as a Christian to experience two things at once. We can be sorrowful in a sense because Christians cry, have regrets, and lose loved ones. Yet in the deepest part of our souls, through the control and power of the Holy Spirit, we can still have joy. We might not show it because of the pain we're experiencing, but inside the joy remains intact.

Because our world has so much discontent and anger, Christians can stand out for the Lord by living joyous lives. The classic biblical example of maintaining joy in the midst of painful circumstances is found in Acts. We read that when the apostle Paul and Silas were in Philippi, they were beaten, flogged, and thrown into prison for no reason. They hadn't done anything wrong. Once in their cell, they could have done anything — planned revenge, cursed the guards, cried for help, or even just paced their cells with fear and worry.

But instead, they were filled with joy. "About midnight Paul and Silas were praying and singing hymns to God, and the other prisoners were listening to them" (Acts 16:25). Not only did they rejoice in the midst of their sorrows, but the other prisoners witnessed their outpouring of joy. The prisoners in the surrounding cells must have thought they were crazy fools to be praising God while under lock and key. But Paul and Silas knew that hardship couldn't take away their joy in Jesus.

"What's Happened to Your Joy?"

Years ago I visited a city in the South and was excited about reconnecting with a Christian woman and her husband who had moved there several years earlier. When the young woman was in her early twenties, she had visited our church and accepted Jesus as her Lord and Savior. Later she was brought to my office where she told me her heartbreaking story. Her own father had abused her, emotionally and sexually. She ended up living in the streets. She worked as a topless dancer, experimented sexually, and eventually got pregnant and had a daughter out of wedlock. She ended up living in a dump of an apartment with no electricity or heat in the Times Square area.

But then she told me about the love of God she had felt while sitting among our congregation as we worshiped God and listened to his Word. She couldn't stop weeping as she realized that Christ was calling her out from her emptiness and depression.

During the next few years, I watched as that young woman blossomed into the most radiant, beautiful Christian woman you could imagine. All the emptiness, the sorrow, the scars, and the things that had weighed down her countenance were replaced by a beautiful joy and the glow of peace. She eventually got married and moved to a different city, but I remembered her joy, and I couldn't wait to see her and her husband again now that I was in town.

But I wasn't in her presence for two minutes when I realized something was wrong. I didn't need any prophetic insight; I could look at her face and tell what happened. I took her aside and asked her what was wrong.

Though the world can't take away our joy, we can still lose it.

"How did you know something was wrong?" she asked.

"Because I can tell by looking at you. You've lost your joy."

She quietly looked downward because she knew it was true.

Though the world can't take away our joy, we can still lose it. In fact, Paul once asked a group of Christians, "What has happened to all your joy?" (Gal. 4:15).[1] That's not the kind of question we typically think to ask of individuals or churches. But when our walk with the Lord gets off track, when we take our eyes off of Jesus, the supernatural joy that only God can give us begins to wane and eventually disappears. We can become sour, depressed, and cranky. We have to ask God to help us if the joy of the Lord is not our daily experience.

Although I never had an opportunity on that trip to talk privately with that woman to know what had caused her to lose her joy, I suspected it had something to do with her family problems. But more importantly, I noticed that after hearing the Word and coming to the altar where we prayed together, she left the church that night with a glow on her face.

Joy in the Spirit

When Christians experience joy today, it has a much more powerful impact on the world than it did decades ago. Why? Because the entitlement mentality so prevalent in our society leads many people to feel justified in their anger. "The government [or my employer, my family — someone for sure!] owes me big-time. I'm entitled because my life has been hard. You have no idea what I've been through." There's often a deep resentment in that kind of complaint. In fact, if you carefully analyze international affairs, national politics, call-in radio shows, blogs, labor disputes, and race relations, there is a worldwide epidemic of venom and bitterness. It's everywhere, and sadly, it has also invaded the body of Christ. It's the exact opposite of the joyous living that Jesus intended for all of us. "I have told you this so that my joy may be in you and that your joy may be complete" (John 15:11).

Centuries before Jesus said those words, joy was already understood as an important facet in the life of God's chosen people. Moses instructed them that the blessings of God were granted so that "your joy will be complete" (Deut. 16:15). Enjoying God's presence produced an even deeper joy than any material blessing (Ps. 21:6), and God's people were to continually celebrate his goodness with "songs of joy" (Ps. 107:22).

When singing a song of joy, it wasn't only the lyrics or melody that made the song worshipful — the singers needed a heart of joy for all that the Lord had done for them. If not, the singing would be unacceptable. God was more interested in joyful hearts than vocal ability. That's why David's attitude pleased God so much. Although surrounded by enemies and under intense stress, David didn't complain, get bitter, or ask, "Why me?" Rather, he went to the tabernacle and made sacrifices with "shouts of joy," saying, "I will sing and make music to the LORD" (Ps. 27:6).

Because of God's faithfulness, the joy in Israel got kind of exuberant at times. Loud singing and shouting were commonplace. They felt joy over the building of the temple, the slaying of Goliath and other military victories, and the exiles returning from captivity. If the Israelites felt that much joy, what kind of joy ought to be present among Christians as we celebrate a crucified and risen Savior? How sad is the dull formalism that characterizes so many of our lives and churches. We have been forgiven, cleansed, justified, and sealed with the Spirit, and we will live eternally with Christ! Aren't joyous singing, shouts of praise, and exuberant thanksgiving in order? I know there's a time to "be still, and know that I am God" (Ps. 46:10), but we should also remember to "sing for joy to God our strength; shout aloud to the God of Jacob" (Ps. 81:1). We're told that God rejoices over us with singing (Zeph. 3:17). The awesome God and creator of all things *rejoices* over me? Well, the least I can do in return is give him the joyful praise he deserves.

The basis of spiritual joy is in our never-changing relationship with Christ. We "rejoice in the Lord" (Phil. 3:1) by remembering and claiming all the benefits he has provided now, and in the hereafter. We all have an unfortunate tendency to dwell exclusively on the problems and pain confronting us, but in Christ, we have a thousand blessings no one can take from us. Jesus said, "You will rejoice, and no one will take away your joy" (John 16:22). Later Paul reinforced Jesus' command by saying, "Rejoice in the Lord always. I will say it again: Rejoice!" (Phil. 4:4). Therefore, we need to resist the "joy thieves" that want to rob us of his precious gift.

In order to keep our joy, we must habitually "rejoice in the Lord," even when we feel nothing or are hurting. It is possible to feel sorrow yet rejoice. To rejoice is to celebrate and glorify Christ *no matter what*. As we do that, the water of the Spirit's joy is drawn up from the well within us.

Many times I have walked into our sanctuary during the praise and worship time distracted and numb, distressed by some crisis or problem. But as I lifted my heart, voice, and hands to my Savior, Jesus Christ, it wasn't long before my heart overflowed with rivers of joy. Through rejoicing in the Lord, my situation didn't change, but my spiritual perspective sure did!

Joy and rejoicing might seem inconsequential to the heady, intellectual types among us. But let's remember how vitally important joy is to our spiritual growth. Paul said: "Convinced of this, I know that I will remain, and I will continue with all of you for *your progress and joy* in the faith" (Phil. 1:25, emphasis added). Paul linked our progress and growth in the faith with the joy that increases as we mature in Christ. Faith grows best in the soil of a heart that rejoices in Jesus despite what's going on around it. That's how David could write some of his most buoyant, joyous psalms while King Saul and the army of Israel were in hot pursuit to destroy him. The prophet Nehemiah said, "The joy of the LORD is [our] strength" (Neh. 8:10). We require that joy for survival. We will never stand victoriously against Satan's daily assaults if our souls are filled with anger and resentment.

The early believers lived precarious lives, never knowing what their allegiance to Jesus might cost them. They faced ten times more difficulties than we do, yet they experienced a hundred times more joy! Let's pray as they did, that God might fill us with joy through the Spirit — not just a momentary pick-me-up from time to time, but a deep and continuous river of joy.

Chapter 9

ENTITLED TO JOY: EVELYN'S STORY

In the preceding chapter, I wrote about how people often feel entitled to their unhappiness because of the life circumstances they've been through. If anyone had a right to feel angry and bitter, it's Evelyn Sanchez. She grew up in poverty, was lied to by the people closest to her, experienced a tragic loss, and at times was so depressed she tried to overdose. So, what is a woman with this kind of tragic past doing now? She's ministering to other women, telling them how they can find joy in their lives. "Happiness depends on happenings, but joy comes from the Lord," is one of her favorite sayings. Despite ongoing trials and tribulations in her life, she is proof that despite our circumstances we can still have joy if we only learn to drink of the Spirit.

EVELYN

I was born on the beautiful island of Puerto Rico, but the story of my birth wasn't so beautiful. My mother wasn't married. When I got older and asked about my father, she told me he was wonderful, but he'd been killed by an evil man before I was born. Though it was hard growing up without a father, I was pleased to know he had been a good man.

When I was two, my mother moved to America seeking a better opportunity for both of us. We settled in the Bronx in an "apartment" that was actually a tiny, windowless room in a cellar. The only portion of the floor that was cemented was the bathroom and kitchen area, which was shared by all the tenants. In our room, the gravel and dirt floor was covered with a combination of cardboard and plastic.

While living there, my mother married and then got pregnant. As soon as the landlord found out she had a baby, he made us move out. He was afraid he'd get in trouble for having a newborn baby living in those conditions.

I was six when we moved to a new place on Dawson Street in the Bronx. I was excited because we finally had windows! Our new home was really a garage located in back of our landlord's property. He'd built three rooms in the upper part of the garage, but there wasn't a bathroom. To use the toilet, we had to go down the stairs, through the backyard, and use the restroom attached to the landlord's house. We had no bathtub or shower. Once a week, my mother warmed water on the stove and filled a tin basin to bathe us.

Our kitchen consisted of a wide porcelain sink with copper faucets. We had an icebox, and ice was delivered twice a week, but there was no hot water and no heat. At night we slept with our coats and gloves on. It was so cold in the winter that if I left a glass of water on the table when I went to bed, in the morning it would be frozen solid.

We had a kerosene heater that my mother was terrified to use at night because she feared it would start a fire. But during the day, we ran it constantly. Unfortunately, it let off a constant stream of black smoke. The soot got into my ears and nostrils and collected under my fingernails. Although I bathed in the basin once a week and had a daily sponge bath, it did little to remove the kerosene residue.

In third grade, we were supposed to come to school each day with a freshly laundered hanky, our hair neatly combed, shoes shined, and fingernails cleaned. One of my classmates, a prim and proper little girl, was appointed monitor. Each day she checked to make sure we all passed her inspection. No matter how hard I tried to clean them, the black sooty stains under my fingernails always got me in trouble. One day I figured out a way to outsmart her. I decided to paint my nails red so she couldn't see the stains anymore. But she was on to me. She told the teacher I painted my nails to hide the dirt, and then she told me I had failed the inspection again. I was humiliated by her daily inspections, but there wasn't anything I could do.

Eventually the garage where we were living needed to be demolished. My uncle helped my mother find an apartment in Hell's Kitchen — a neighborhood on the west side of Manhattan. When I learned that we were moving, I couldn't have been happier! I wanted to get away from Miss Prim and her daily inspections. I bragged to all my friends how we were moving to the city. Our apartment was about three blocks from Times Square, and I was ecstatic about living near all of those lights and theaters.

I was nine, my brother was five, and my mother was pregnant with my sister when we moved into the six-family brick building on 44th Street. In our new home, the kids all shared one bedroom. It was really more like a closet, but I didn't care, because it had bunk beds and a dresser with four drawers! Since I was the oldest, I claimed two drawers for myself, leaving my siblings with one each. My mother and stepfather slept in the living room. We still didn't have heat or hot water, so we continued to use the kerosene lamps and heaters. But we did have a kitchen with a refrigerator. And the bathroom was on the same floor, just down the hall.

> **I didn't have much of a childhood because I had to assume grown-up responsibilities very early in life.**

I didn't have much of a childhood because I had to assume grown-up responsibilities very early in life. My mother couldn't speak English, and her reading and writing abilities in Spanish were limited since she had only a fourth-grade education. Though she was a beautiful, hardworking woman, she relied on me to help her with the world outside of our home, and whenever she went out, I had to translate for her. While I always knew my mother loved me, she never told me, except once, on my wedding day and only after I asked. She wasn't very affectionate, and I don't remember her ever holding me, kissing me, or hugging me. But I knew she must have loved me, because she took such good care of me.

My little sister, Nellie, was my biggest joy in life. She was like my little doll. I would dress her, bathe her, and play with her hair. She was my pride and joy. Nellie was the only thing that mattered to me and the only loving, intimate relationship I had growing up. She was the only one I hugged and kissed and who hugged and kissed me back. She was my ball of joy.

While living in Hell's Kitchen, we started visiting a small Spanish church. There I learned about Jesus, and I watched as my mother gave her heart to the Lord. Nellie also loved the Lord. Much to my delight, and I am sure to his, she sang songs and praises to him.

When I was ten, I learned my older cousin would be going to Puerto Rico for her summer vacation. I wanted to go in the worst way, and eventually I talked my mother into letting me go. While at my cousin's house talking with her excitedly and making preparations for our upcoming trip, my uncle came in and said to me, "Now, you can finally meet your father."

"My father is dead," I said. "He was killed by a bad man."

"No, he's not. Your mother has been lying to you." Then he handed me a piece of paper. "Here is his name, the address where he lives, and the place where he works. When you go there, make sure you visit him."

I felt as if I had been stabbed in the heart. My father was still alive? I had been lied to all these years? All the way home, I cried bitter tears of anger.

At home I confronted my mother. "Is this true?"

"Why would I tell you about a man who wanted nothing to do with you? He wouldn't even give you his name!" I saw pain in her eyes, but I persisted.

"But he's my father!"

Over the next few days as we prepared for our trip, I became more and more excited about the possibility of meeting my father. What would he be like? Would he be handsome or maybe even rich?

Through various relatives, I pieced together the story of what had happened. My mother came from the wrong side of the tracks in Puerto Rico. Her family was poor and not well educated. My father came from the other side. His family had more money and thought they were better than my mother and her family. So my father's family was not happy when she got pregnant. They pressured my father to stay away and not have anything else to do with her. He even went so far as to deny that I was his child, so he was out of the picture well before I was even born. Obviously my mother had been very hurt by the things he had said and done. Telling me he was dead was the best way she knew to leave her heartache in the past.

I was pretty independent and headstrong as a kid. Once I arrived in Puerto Rico, the first chance I got I went straight to my father's place of employment. He was a DJ at the only radio station in the town, so everyone knew him. At the station, I introduced myself to the woman behind the desk and told her why I was there. She immediately kicked me out of the station and told me never to come back. I later learned she was his wife.

Outside, I sat on the curb and wept uncontrollably while my cousin stood by unsure of what to do. I had been so excited to finally meet my father, and an uncaring secretary had dashed all my dreams and ended my hopes for a reunion. A woman who was walking by stopped, leaned over me, and asked, "Little girl, why are you crying? What's wrong?"

Apparently she thought I was lost or hurt. My cousin spoke up. "She came all the way from New York to see her father, and the secretary in there told her she couldn't come in and kicked her out."

"Well, you come with me," said the woman as she grabbed my hand and led me down the street to the police station. We entered the building, and without talking to anyone, she took me straight back to the captain's office and told him what happened. The captain stood up. He was so big he looked like a lion, and at first I was scared.

"We'll take care of it," he told the lady.

He ordered a policeman to take me back to the radio station. Together, the policeman and I walked right in. When the secretary saw me with him, she got all shook up. He sat me down and then motioned for her to come and speak with him privately. When they finished, she went into the studio and brought out my father.

Seeds were planted that day that would find root and grow over the next few years.

When he walked into the room and his eyes found mine, we stared for a minute. *He looks just like me,* I thought. I could tell from the expression on his face that he thought the same thing. I stared into his eyes, and in my naïveté, I really believed he would pick me up in his strong arms, swing me around, kiss me, and tell me how glad he was to see me.

Instead, he said, "What are you doing here? Where is your mother?"

"She's in New York. I'm here on vacation."

"Okay, great. I can't talk to you; I am very busy right now, but I will dedicate a song to you on the radio." Then he turned and disappeared back inside the studio. I never saw him again.

I left the station hurt and angry. Seeds were planted that day that would find root and grow over the next few years. My fantasy over the previous weeks had been that I would find a loving father, but my dreams of being loved by a father died that day.

Now all I had was Nellie.

A couple of years later, I was at home one evening helping Mom make dinner when Nellie called through the window, "Evelyn, I love you. I love you!"

"I love you too," I called back.

"I want to go to Lenny's house," she said.

Lenny was her Caucasian friend who often came over to our house, and she went to his. They were the best of friends and loved to play together. The homes on our street were all four-story, six-family homes, and Lenny lived only seven or eight houses up the street from us.

"Okay," I said, leaning out the window so she could see me. "But tell Lenny's mom to send you home at six." I held up six fingers. "Six o'clock you need to come home for dinner, okay?" She nodded and then skipped off toward Lenny's.

It was the last time I ever spoke to her.

While playing indoors at Lenny's house, they were seated on the window frame of an open window. Though the window had been fitted with child guard rails, the frame had rotted and the rails weren't secure. When the kids leaned into it, the rails gave way. Nellie fell from the second-story window to the pavement below. Lenny fell next and, according to an eyewitness, landed on Nellie before bouncing onto the grass. Lenny's eighteen-month-old brother also went through the window but got his legs entangled in the rails. He dangled precariously as onlookers watched in horror until his mother was able to save him. Both boys survived, but an ambulance came and took Nellie to the hospital. Police and firefighters were there to investigate. My mother went home to get my stepfather so they could go to the hospital together, but I couldn't wait for her. I rode to the hospital with a reporter from *The Daily Mirror*, and once there, I snuck into the ER and found Nellie's room.

She was unconscious — so still and quiet as she lay on the table. "Nellie, wake up! Wake up, Nellie!" I begged, crying.

But a nurse heard me and came running. "You can't be in here," she said, and she forced me to leave.

My older cousin joined me in the waiting room. Nellie lived six hours from the time of the accident. They tried to operate, but she didn't make it through the surgery. I was the one who had to break the news to my mother and stepfather. Something in my heart died with Nellie.

My mother refused to return to our apartment. Instead, family picked us up at the hospital, and we went to Brooklyn to stay with my cousins. We never went back to our home in Manhattan. My mother wouldn't speak of Nellie, and she wouldn't keep any photos of her. I had to hide the few pictures I had so she wouldn't throw them away. Mother didn't want anything around that reminded her of her deceased daughter.

When I was fourteen, we finally moved for the first time into an apartment that had heat and hot water. There was also a bathtub and a shower! At night after everyone else was asleep, I would fill the tub with hot water and soak in it, refilling it as the water leaked out or became cold. I loved feeling surrounded by water and stayed in until my skin wrinkled. Sometimes I held my nose and slipped beneath the surface, staying down for as long as I could. I just wanted to feel the embrace and warmth of the water.

I blamed myself for Nellie's death. If she hadn't been at Lenny's, she wouldn't have fallen out of the window. No one talked to me about her death. No one told me it wasn't my fault. So there was no one I could tell about the guilt I carried. I began a downward spiral in my life — rebelling, acting out, doing poorly in school, and hanging with the wrong crowd. Nellie was the only one in my life whom I really loved who was able to love me back. Now she was gone, and it was my fault.

My anger toward God grew to hate. Why were the little boys spared? Their parents were atheists. My mother was a Christian, and my sister loved the Lord! God was supposed to protect her and

My mother assumed that either the devil was responsible for my behavior or God was trying to get my attention.

take care of her — at least that's what they taught us at church. But he didn't take care of Nellie. So I turned my back on him. "I don't want to know you. I don't want anything to do with you," I told him. Losing my sister caused me to run away from God while my mother drew closer to him.

I was fourteen when I took an overdose of aspirin and then went to school. I figured I would die there and make a big scene. Everyone would know. But I started to nod off in my English class, and they took me to the nurse's station. I was cold and clammy. The nurse thought I was on drugs and sent me to the hospital. My cousin met me there. Fortunately, she was able to tell them what had been going on. I narrowly escaped having to be locked up in the mental ward.

My mother assumed that either the devil was responsible for my behavior or God was trying to get my attention. "You're such a mocker," she would say when I told her I didn't want anything to do with God. "When God gets ahold of you, the Holy Spirit is going to grab you by the hair and drag you all the way down to the altar." Her description of God and the Holy Spirit only made me want to stay away from them both.

At sixteen I was looking for someone to care for me and someone who would love me, so I married a man ten years older. At first he treated me like I was his little princess. But the following year, I gave birth to my son, Jose. Once Jose was born, I turned my attention and affection toward him, and my husband became jealous. One night he got so drunk that he took Jose by one arm and flung him against the wall. We were living with my mother at the time, and when she heard the commotion followed by Jose's sudden screams of pain, she came running. She broke down the locked door and called the cops.

I was divorced by the time I was twenty.

A year later, I got married a second time, and a year after that I had my daughter, Melissa. When she was seven, I gave birth to Ricardo. My new marriage wasn't much better than my first. My second husband was also an alcoholic.

Shortly after Ricardo's birth, I started visiting my mother's church. She had been taking my kids even when I didn't go, but I knew something needed to change in my life, and I was finally ready. Over time, despite my anger, I slowly began to feel as though God was speaking to me, gently drawing me closer to him.

One day, while showering and getting dressed, I thought, *I can't believe I'm getting dressed on New Year's Eve to go to church! Maybe I should make a New Year's resolution and give my life to Christ. People say he fills your life with love, joy, and peace. Maybe I should give him an opportunity to do that in my life.*

At the service that night, the pastor asked those who wanted to give their lives to Christ to come forward. I stayed in my seat. Then he said, "The Holy Spirit is telling me that someone here is battling. Why don't you give God an opportunity? Why don't you make Christ your New Year's resolution? Why don't you see if he can give you the joy, peace, and love that you crave in your life?"

That's when I got up from my seat and dashed to the altar.

I gave my life to Christ that night, and when I did, I remember feeling submerged in his love just like I used to submerge myself in a warm bath. His love completely surrounded me. The Holy Spirit didn't drag me down the aisle, and God wasn't angry. I felt only love.

After that I went from being angry and bitter and wanting to kill myself to knowing what real peace, love, and joy were all about. My circumstances hadn't changed; I was still in a loveless marriage. But now I had a desire to make my marriage work, to serve God, and to create a loving, Christ-centered home for my family.

I can't tell you how dramatic the change was. I had been a very vengeful person. If you said two nasty words to me, I spat back five, making sure mine were last. And I hated my stepfather so badly that I couldn't even look at him. When I no longer felt that way, I knew that by God's grace I had become a new person in Christ and had been delivered from my anger and bitterness. I went from merely existing to having an abundant life, and I wanted to share that feeling with others. I enrolled in a neighborhood Bible school so I could learn the Word of God.

Around this time, I started coming to the Brooklyn Tabernacle. I had never seen a church with greater joy, and I learned even more about how joy was linked to the Holy Spirit. I discovered a verse in Zephaniah that changed the way I thought about God: "He will take great delight in you; in his love he will no longer rebuke you, but will rejoice over you with singing" (Zeph. 3:17). *Oh God! Not only have you taught me to rejoice, but you also rejoice over me? I bring joy to your heart? And you rejoice over me with singing?* I didn't know my earthly father, but now I knew my heavenly Father loved me and rejoiced over me!

I volunteered at church for years and eventually got a full-time job, and now I've worked there for nearly thirty years. Today I am the director of women's ministries. I teach the Bible and disciple believers in Jesus. Every day I counsel women and remind them that joy is from the Lord. It is a gift of God that no one can take away. I want them to know that their mistakes (like mine) aren't final. Our God is a living God, a God who restores what Satan has stolen and gives us a new start in life.

Becoming a Christian didn't make my life perfect or perfectly happy. My marriage remained rocky despite my best intentions. When my husband turned my youngest son against me, and nothing I did or said fixed things, God gave me a verse, "The LORD will fight for you; you need only to be still" (Ex. 14:14), and I learned to trust him in new ways. Eventually my husband and I divorced, and my son and I have reconciled. But even today I still have battles that try to steal my joy. A person I love dearly has turned his back on the Lord, and this past year my mother died.

The Christian life is a choice, and I choose daily to remain in his presence.

The Christian life is a choice, and I choose daily to remain in his presence. I practice joy by being thankful and grateful for all that has been given to me. And I find joy in the fact that I am still learning and growing. I know that a lot of people feel entitled to hang on to their anger and bitterness. I believe in entitlements too. I am a child of God, and I am entitled to his love, peace, and joy, and most of all his grace. I want every good thing he has planned for me.

Chapter 10

THERE IS A QUEST FOR CHRISTLIKENESS

Nicole Crews grew up in Germany with an African-American father and a German mother who divorced when Nicole was very young. Her mother drank — a lot. Living with an alcoholic was difficult, and Nicole had to shoulder many family responsibilities for her and her brother. Unfortunately, when Nicole was only seventeen, her mother died.

Nicole was tall and beautiful, and she started modeling at fifteen. She enjoyed a lot of success in Germany, but at twenty-five she decided to move to Miami and work for an agent representing her there. "After some time in Miami, I realized the lifestyle there was different than I expected," Nicole said. "There was a lot of partying, and I thought it was too distracting and too dangerous. So I moved to New York." (I have to say, Nicole is the only person I can recall who ever moved to New York City for safety reasons!)

Though she didn't grow up in church, most people still would have described Nicole as a "good girl." She didn't drink or use drugs, because she saw what happened to her mother. But she liked to go clubbing and dancing. As a model, she could get into the best clubs and was invited to A-list parties. But she was also focused on her career. "I was totally aiming to be a Victoria's Secret model."

Though her career was successful, Nicole felt empty. She asked around about churches, and eventually another model brought her to our church. "I was always searching," Nicole said. "In Germany we heard about gospel choirs and how they were funky and upbeat, and so I was always drawn to that. I came to the Brooklyn Tabernacle because I wanted to hear good music."

The first Sunday she attended, we showed a video of our ministry in Haiti, and it awakened something in Nicole. She came back the next Sunday, and then the next. "Then one Sunday in June of 2006, I was sitting in the balcony, and Pastor Cymbala kind of looked up, and while I don't remember what he said, I felt like he was talking to me. I was crying, and I turned to look at another model friend I was with, and she was crying too. And I just knew I needed to go down front and pray to accept Jesus as my Lord and Savior."

During the next year, Nicole continued to go on casting calls, take modeling assignments, dance at clubs, and attend industry parties. But she also came to church on Sunday, attended prayer meetings during the week, and took Bible classes. "But something didn't line up," Nicole said. "I kept reading the Word about what made a righteous life, but I wasn't living it. Things I learned in my Bible class kept convicting me." Inside she began to feel differently about situations that had never bothered her before.

"The last party I went to was on Halloween night in 2007. I got all dressed up and was excited to go. But within ten minutes after arriving, I found myself looking at all the crazy stuff going on around me — drugs, alcohol, homosexuality, casual sex, and just weird stuff. I looked at what my friends were doing, and I thought, *I don't belong here.* I knew then it was totally the Holy Spirit, because I wasn't doing anything wrong. I don't drink and I don't smoke. But suddenly I realized this wasn't the scene for me. So I left and never went back to that lifestyle."

Nicole began to feel the Holy Spirit prodding her about other issues. "One day I got dressed and I looked at myself in the mirror and thought, *Why do these clothes look weird?*" She changed the way she dressed. Necklines came up, T-shirts and jeans weren't as tight, and she covered more skin. "As I felt God's conviction, I got rid of things in my life. I became more modest in the way I dressed. No one told me to do it. It just happened over time."

Nicole modeled lingerie and swimwear, and it had never bothered her. But once again she felt a gentle tug on her conscience. "One day

I was modeling lingerie, and I suddenly realized it was all about sex appeal. It's all about sex, sex, sex. It hadn't dawned on me before, because it was just a normal part of the industry. The Holy Spirit was telling me that there was something wrong with these kinds of shoots."

Though Nicole worked for an agency that was responsible for sending her out on jobs, she decided she could no longer do certain shoots. "I knew I needed to talk to the booker who sent me on jobs, but I hated to confront her about this because it could be a career killer. But finally, I did. I just sat down and told her that some of the jobs were starting to make me feel weird and awkward."

When Nicole was asked to do a print job for a skin product, she agreed. The plan was to shoot body parts — arms, legs, and hands — of several women of different skin colors. "What I didn't know was that the models had to be completely nude in front of the photographer. I was so humiliated and felt so degraded, that by September, I officially retired."

> **When the Spirit starts his work, we will *always* have a new desire for holiness and a quest for Christlikeness.**

Holy, separated living isn't preached about much anymore because we fear it might offend and not be visitor-friendly. But when the Spirit starts his work, we will *always* have a new desire for holiness and a quest for Christlikeness. "As obedient children, do not conform to the evil desires you had when you lived in ignorance. But just as he who called you is holy, so be holy in all you do; for it is written: 'Be holy, because I am holy'" (1 Peter 1:14 – 16).

Nicole believes that not every Christian is called to leave the modeling industry; she still has Christian friends who have made it work. But for her, God had different plans. "The Holy Spirit kept refining me, and I definitely felt like God was testing me to see how strong my faith was." Nicole continued to make big and small changes based on her renewed mind as God's Spirit applied Scripture. As she learned more, more godly changes came about in her lifestyle.

The word *holy* speaks of separation and purity. It must be important to God, for he tells us that "without holiness no one will see the Lord" (Heb. 12:14). Holiness is not a list of dos and don'ts. Rather, it is Christlikeness. As the Spirit works, we will have an increased desire to be holy like Christ. What else would the Holy Spirit do but impart his own nature into our lives?

The Battle between Flesh and Spirit

Nicole's testimony is a great example of how once we trust Christ for salvation, God will begin to mold and shape us. Many of us have experienced similar radical changes when we first came to know Christ. But over time, a battle between our flesh and the Spirit takes place inside of us. The apostle Paul wrote, "For the flesh desires what is contrary to the Spirit, and the Spirit what is contrary to the flesh. They are in conflict with each other, so that you are not to do whatever you want" (Gal. 5:17). Paul was writing to the saints ("holy ones") in Galatia, but he acknowledged that they, like him, had to overcome a carnal undertow from inside that pulled against the Spirit's purposes.

What is it about the flesh that is so contrary to the Spirit?

Paul continued: "The acts of the flesh are obvious: sexual immorality, impurity and debauchery; idolatry and witchcraft; hatred, discord, jealousy, fits of rage, selfish ambition, dissensions, factions and envy; drunkenness, orgies, and the like" (Gal. 5:19–21). That's a pretty nasty list of sinful behaviors. And it's the perpetual output of the flesh; in fact, it's all our fallen natures can ever produce. While we won't individually practice all the sins listed, the teaching of Scripture is clear: left to himself without the Spirit's grace, all Jim Cymbala will do is indulge the "flesh" and live a life of self-gratification.

That's precisely why Paul started his comments about the flesh by saying: "You, my brothers and sisters, were called to be free. But do not use your freedom to *indulge* the flesh; rather, serve one another humbly in love" (Gal. 5:13, emphasis added). What were they free from? They were free from the law — trying to earn acceptance with God by obeying the law. The Galatians had already accepted Jesus Christ as the sacrificial substitute for their sins. But this free gift of salvation must not lead to a life of indulging the sinful nature. Besides, how could they go back to doing the very things for which Christ died on the cross?

Some may argue that is not what Paul meant or that once we accept Christ as our Savior, Christians no longer have natural sinful tendencies. But Paul wasn't the only one who cautioned about sinful practices in the lives of believers. John also reminded us of this truth: "My dear children, I write this to you so that you will not sin. But if anybody does sin, we have an advocate with the Father — Jesus Christ, the Righteous One" (1 John 2:1). John's intention was plain — to inspire God's people not to practice unrighteousness but to practice Christlike living. The Holy Spirit brings new sensitivities and convictions to us if we are really living under his control. Behavior, words, and attitudes that are unholy cause a reaction from the Spirit who is holy. In fact, Christians living loose, carnal lives are usually joyless and lacking peace. The Spirit is sending out all kinds of cautions, warnings, and red alerts to bring us back to following Christ's example.

Unseen Dirt

The more Nicole's mind was renewed (Rom. 12:2), the more new convictions brought about a greater Christlikeness in her. And that process never ends while we live on earth. The more we draw near to God and desire to live a life pleasing to him, the more we see things we never saw before.

One day I was at home sitting in the study outside of my bedroom. It was summer, and the blinds were open and the bright morning sun shone through the slats. I was talking to someone on the phone, and I remember a direct beam of sunshine, an incredibly bright ray of light, was focused on my knee. When the caller said something funny, I laughed and slapped my knee. As soon as I hit my pants, a cloud of something, dust maybe, sprung up. I was wearing a pair of freshly laundered Dockers, yet a battalion of microparticles had been camping out in my pants! I had slapped my leg many times before, and there was probably a cloud every time I did it, but until that day, I had never seen it before. Only through the intense light could I see the microscopic dust on my apparently clean pants.

The Holy Spirit is like that light. We may think we are doing just fine, but when that Light shines on us, we see lots of things we never saw before. As the Holy Spirit gains more control of our lives, as with Nicole, we gain a new perspective on sin. Things that didn't used to bother us suddenly do. We become convicted about things that seemed fine earlier in our Christian walk.

If a person doesn't have a growing sensitivity toward sin and doesn't have a desire to become more like Christ, it's questionable whether that person ever had an authentic conversion. False conversions do take place. It's possible to have mental affirmation that there is a God and that Jesus is his Son. According to James, even the demons believe that (James 2:19). But in a true spiritual conversion, we will always see tenderness of heart, a new reliance on Christ, and a desire to be more like him. That has been the pattern for more than two thousand years. Recognizing our sin isn't enough. Grieving over it proves God is at work.

Good Grief

The Spirit is present in our life when we realize "I can't do that anymore" and cry out for victory over besetting sin. But we also know the Helper is present when we fail and feel a deep remorse. No true child of God can casually practice unrighteousness without eventual pangs of guilt and a desperate craving for cleansing.

Consider Peter. He belonged to Jesus and was a leading disciple, yet Peter denied the Lord three times. After the denials, Peter went off into the night weeping. Why did he weep? Was he afraid he would lose his standing as a disciple? No, Peter didn't lose his relationship with Jesus in that moment. But Peter did acutely feel the pain of his betrayal and the loss of fellowship with someone he loved deeply. The Spirit was working to bring the pain that leads to repentance and restoration.

Paul warned, "Do not grieve the Holy Spirit of God" (Eph. 4:30). If the Spirit is grieved, he's vexed and sad. Although we know our salvation isn't lost by our sin, we also become painfully aware that there's a strain in our relationship. Communion with God is affected, and we feel an uncomfortable emptiness. The sun is still there and shining, but we no longer feel its warmth. It is as if a cloud blocks it.

> The Spirit is present in our life when we realize "I can't do that anymore" and cry out for victory over besetting sin.

One of the deepest pains we can feel is when we break communion with someone we love. That can happen between spouses, siblings, or friends. We suffer deeply when, because of a misunderstanding or argument, we suddenly damage a relationship with someone we have walked with, talked with, and laughed with.

Sin ruptures our fellowship with God. Our disobedience breaks communion with him and brings spiritual loss. But that pain of conviction can also be used for good as we grow closer to Christ and ask God for grace to rid ourselves of the sinful things.

What *should* we do about our ongoing battles with the flesh? If we continue to draw closer to Christ, we become more intent on being like him. But consciousness of our daily failings can also trigger the worst possible response — *trying harder* to overcome the works of the flesh and be more like Christ. It is an impossible task, because how can I cast out myself?

Stepping Out with the Spirit

Paul gave the only answer to our dilemma: "So I say, *walk by the Spirit,* and you will not gratify the desires of the flesh" (Gal. 5:16, emphasis added). Sounds simple, doesn't it? Just walk by the Spirit. Problem solved! But how in the world do you apply a verse like that? How do you walk in the Spirit? What does that look like on a daily basis?

We can picture what it meant to walk with Jesus. The disciples did that. If Jesus stayed in Capernaum for five days, they stayed in Capernaum for five days. If Jesus stopped for lunch, they stopped for lunch. If he turned to the right and went down the road, they followed behind him. But how do we do that with the invisible Holy Spirit? Some might say, "Just go by the Word." But it's that very Word that tells us to walk by the Spirit. Filling our hearts with Scripture builds faith and encourages us. But here we're told that following the Spirit and keeping in step with him is the only deliverance from indulging our lower nature and its ugly potential. How do we do that?

First of all, reliance on the Spirit means we have his help in repenting of those sins that so easily attach themselves to us. Many believers lie to themselves and are in denial as to the "secret treaty" they've made with disobedience. The Holy Spirit alone can help us keep real with God. Whether we struggle with overt wrong actions or subtler unchristlike attitudes, the Spirit's light focuses directly on the infection and helps us sincerely turn away from it. Repentance is a 180-degree U-turn from sin and selfishness back to God.

Walking by the Spirit is a twenty-four-hour-a-day, seven-day-a-week lifestyle. It's not about going to church on Sundays. It requires much prayer and sensitivity. Unlike Jesus' physical movements and audible words, the Spirit's work is accomplished through our yield-edness to his prompting and movement. He wants to work in the deepest level of our being — the place where our thoughts, desires, and plans are formed. That is why Paul wrote, "Continue to work out your salvation with fear and trembling, for it is God who works in you to *will* and to *act* in order to fulfill his good purpose" (Phil. 2:12 – 13, emphasis added). By yielding to the Spirit's precious work, he influences the formation of desires within us, deadening our selfish tendencies toward sin. We overcome the lower nature not by fighting against it ourselves — a losing battle if there ever was one — but by allowing the Holy Spirit to exert his power, every second of the day, on our behalf. In fact, the only one who can put the flesh to death is the Spirit of life.

Charles Finney wrote:

> If you mean to [be filled with] the Spirit, you must be childlike, and yield to His influences — just as yielding as air. If He is drawing you to prayer, you must quit everything to yield to His gentle strivings. No doubt you have sometimes felt a desire to pray for some object, and you have put it off and resisted, until God left you. If you wish Him to remain, you must yield to His softest leadings, watch to learn what He would have you do and yield yourself up to His guidance.

A Christlike life is a mystery. We live the life — it's our voice, body, and mind — but it's not really us at all. It's Christ living in us through the Holy Spirit. But that can't be learned and put into practice overnight. Every believer has experienced the tears of regret when our flesh reasserts itself and we do and say things that we know are wrong. But John, the same apostle who wrote a letter to encourage believers not to sin, also included one of the best promises in the Bible: "If we claim to be without sin, we deceive ourselves and the truth is not in us. *If we confess our sins*, he is faithful and just and will forgive us our sins and purify us from all unrighteousness" (1 John 1:8 – 9).

Many years ago I attended a Bible conference in upstate New York. I was new to the ministry and hungry to learn. The teaching sessions were fine, but I learned the most valuable lesson while walking to lunch. The main speaker, a seasoned man of God, was walking with an associate in front of my friend and me. "You want to know something?" he said within earshot. "To be conscious of the Holy Spirit solves 90 percent of our problems." That was his little nugget, and it has stayed with me ever since. The key is to be aware of and in touch with the Spirit.

A Christlike life is a mystery. We live the life — it's our voice, body, and mind — but it's not really us at all.

The Bible declares that a Christian is a new creation (2 Cor. 5:17). Christ's plan was to replace "me" with "him" through the Spirit's presence. That is a far more radical idea than starting to attend church more regularly or reading the Bible occasionally. It's more of a "corporate takeover." But the takeover results in a life filled with peace and joy.

Keep in Step with the Spirit

Most of us started our Christian lives with the belief that God was all we needed. Period. Certainly we knew we had no part in gaining acceptance with God. His salvation was a free gift — all we had done was to believe and receive. But then following Christ got a little more complicated. Aware of our failings, we turned not to him but to ourselves! That's why Paul summarized his teaching to the Galatians in these words: "Since we *live by* the Spirit, let us keep *in step with* the Spirit" (Gal. 5:25, emphasis added).

We are born again through the Holy Spirit in us, and we live by the Spirit. Having begun that way, should we now revert back to self-effort in our pathetic attempts to live good lives? Paul's directive is to *keep in step with the Spirit* — the living presence of God dwelling in our hearts. Just as Nicole had to keep in step with the Spirit as God peeled off layer after layer of stuff displeasing to him, we must allow God to do the same. The work goes on, not only for Nicole, but for all of us.

In our own strength, we can never act like Jesus Christ. That's why he sent us a Helper. The Spirit of Jesus within us wants to tenderly and lovingly manage our days. This isn't a bad thing. He wasn't sent to rain on our parade and hinder us from enjoying the best of life. Just the opposite. He is ready and able to lead us out into the clean, fresh air of Christlike words, thoughts, and actions.

Lord, we want to be holy like you.

[Chapter 11]

THERE IS POWER

As we were praying at the end of our first service on a recent Sunday, I met an older woman who had come to the altar area at the front of the sanctuary. While trying to encourage her, I learned she was a grandmother who lived in a one-bedroom apartment in a troubled area of Brooklyn. She was experiencing some very deep waters, indeed. As I talked with her more, I learned she had a grown daughter who had been in and out of a mental institution. That daughter had two teenage sons, and the three of them lived with the grandmother. A second daughter, who had a six-year-old child, lived in her small apartment as well. But that wasn't all; I was shocked to learn about a grown son who also called her apartment home. Eight people lived in her tiny one-bedroom apartment!

Earlier in the week, the authorities had come to the apartment and notified her that her teenage grandsons had been molesting the six-year-old granddaughter. The grandmother's heart was broken. She loved Jesus and was fighting desperately for her family.

I prayed with all my heart for her and then brought in our family ministries director. What a brave woman to hang on to God's promises in the midst of such depressing chaos!

At the second service, a teenage girl came to the altar and prayed. Tears glistened at the corners of her closed eyes. I waited for the right moment to talk with her, but even after I dismissed those who had to go, she continued to pray. While the musicians continued to softly play for those who remained in the sanctuary, I put my hand on her arm, a fatherly sign that she wasn't alone. She suddenly began to sob from some deep place inside of her. It was so deep that, frankly, it alarmed me. Standing next to her, I silently prayed, *God, come and comfort her. Holy Spirit, guide me. What should I do? What should I say?*

I let more time pass, then finally I asked her to sit down on the steps in the front of the church so we could talk.

"How old are you?" I asked.

"Fourteen," she said, but she looked much older. She told me her name and a few other details.

Finally, I asked, "What's troubling you? What's wrong?"

Tentatively at first, she told me her story. For the past three years, her stepfather had been molesting her. Finally, someone had called the authorities, and they were going to arrest him, but they hadn't picked him up yet. He was still out there, and she was frightened.

About that time, I looked up and saw her mother standing over us both. She was a lovely lady with tear-filled eyes. It was their first visit to our church, and God was dealing in love with both of them.

"Is it true what your daughter's been telling me?" I asked.

"Yes," she answered with deep emotion.

"Where do you live?"

"We live in a shelter in another borough of the city."

I took them up to my office, and while there I led both of them in a prayer to get their relationship right with God through Jesus Christ. Others brought them over to our hospitality area for lunch. They stayed with me the entire day. We prayed, *God, show us the way out of this shelter, and show us where we're supposed to go from here.*

What Are We to Do?

Well, you can imagine after hearing those stories after the first two services, I wasn't sure what to expect after the third! Anyone who has worked in ministry has probably had a day like that. But we don't even have to be officially in ministry to find ourselves in the middle of someone else's heartbreaking problems. Perhaps something is going on in your family, or a coworker has shared a personal struggle.

Maybe one of your own kids is rebelling, or the bottom has somehow fallen out of your life.

On Tuesday nights, our prayer meeting begins at seven, but the doors open two hours earlier for those who desire extra time with God. Recently I entered the sanctuary around six to pray for those with special needs. I stood in the front along with other pastors, deacons, and Prayer Band members as we helped a long line of people requesting prayer. I must have prayed for at least a dozen people. One first-time visitor was depressed because her marriage was falling apart, but she also told me she was having an ongoing affair with her previous boyfriend. Another woman had a test coming up to get higher medical credentials, but currently she was out of work and living in a shelter. A third person was struggling in her efforts to quit smoking. Another person was concerned about her son who was serving a sentence of up to thirty years in an upstate penitentiary.

There are days I have to pray to God just to ask him *how* I should pray!

When we are confronted with people who have such desperate needs, what should we do? I always want to pray for people who are hurting, but sometimes I am not even sure what or how to pray. There are days I have to pray to God just to ask him *how* I should pray!

When critical situations arise and I come to the end of my abilities, I deeply feel my inadequacy. Something more is needed. But more of what? Not more praise and worship choruses — I know tons of those. Not a better translation of the Bible. Do I need a degree in counseling? No, most of all I need power from heaven. If we want to spread the gospel and see Christ-glorifying conversions, if we want to see breakthroughs in difficult — even seemingly impossible — situations, we must have more power from the Holy Spirit. Without Holy Spirit power, we'll never have enough of what we need to become the people God wants us to be.

THE MESSAGE ALONE IS NOT ENOUGH

I love to look at the buildings of Manhattan, especially at night when the lights are all on. It's an amazing sight to see all of those buildings filled with people, activities, and ideas at work, and to know that what is hatched there will not only affect New York City but the entire world. However, regardless of how influential New York City and its people can be, if you take away the electrical power — which happens occasionally during a blackout — the whole thing shuts down. The office buildings become useless, the activity ceases, and the ideas die in the darkness. Without power, all that potential is wasted.

The same is true for us believers. If we don't have access to spiritual power, how can we accomplish what needs to be done? Power to overcome sin. Power to overcome spiritual enemies that attack us. Power to endure hardship and affliction. Power to witness. Power to speak. Power to pray. Isn't more spiritual power probably the greatest need we have today?

It's interesting that the risen Christ's final words before his ascension concerned spiritual power. "I am going to send you what my Father has promised; but stay in the city until you have been clothed with *power* from on high" (Luke 24:49, emphasis added). It was as if Jesus looked down the corridors of time and knew that even having the right gospel message wouldn't be enough. We would face so many such obstacles from satanic strongholds that we would never evangelize the world effectively without the power that only the Spirit can impart.

Think about the situation the disciples were in. They had been with Jesus who had risen from the dead. And for the first time, they finally understood the meaning of the sacrifice he made on the cross, the blood that was shed for the remission of all sins. They had seen the nail marks in his hands. They had seen him ascend into heaven. Imagine how badly they must have wanted to tell people about what they saw! Think of the excitement when they finally understood the good news. They felt the desperate spiritual state of those in Judea, Samaria, and Galilee, as well as the rest of the world. *Let's start this evangelizing business right now,* they must have thought. *Let's get the message out. We're wasting valuable time.*

We might even think that Jesus would agree with that kind of thinking. That he'd say, "Okay, now that you've seen the nail marks and you know I'm alive, go out and preach the message!" But he didn't. He told them to do the exact opposite of what they were inclined to do. Jesus told them to wait.

BRAINS AND TALENT WON'T BE ENOUGH

Jesus knew far better than the disciples did that the equipment needed for the job was more than keen intellect, human talent, and even a sincere heart. So they obediently did as Jesus said. They waited in the upper room praying, singing, and praising God. "When the day of Pentecost came, they were all together in one place. Suddenly a sound like the blowing of a violent wind came from heaven and filled the whole house where they were sitting. They saw what seemed to be tongues of fire that separated and came to rest on each of them.

We all know about Peter's failings as a disciple, but let's be honest—the others weren't much better.

All of them were filled with the Holy Spirit and began to speak in other tongues as the Spirit enabled them" (Acts 2:1 – 4).

The Spirit was poured out just as Jesus promised. What the prophet Joel predicted had happened. "In the last days, God says, I will pour out my Spirit on all people. Your sons and daughters will prophesy, your young men will see visions, your old men will dream dreams" (Acts 2:17 – 21). This meant that a new kind of ability was available. "[For] you will receive power *when* the Holy Spirit comes on you" (Acts 1:8, emphasis added). This awesome power from heaven was needed on earth to build Christ's kingdom.

Were those disciples sincere believers in Jesus as they waited in Jerusalem? Yes. Did they have correct doctrine? Yes. Could they have gone out and preached without the Holy Spirit? I am sure they wanted to, but Jesus knew they were not ready. He knew the power of the enemy they would face, the discouragements, and the opposition. If the Holy Spirit's power was needed then, has anything changed to this very day? Will anything else but the Spirit's power working through us pull down the walls of unbelief and break the powers of compulsive sinful behavior as we share the gospel?

We all know about Peter's failings as a disciple, but let's be honest — the others weren't much better. They weren't educated people. Jesus could have asked twelve rabbis to be his followers, but he didn't. He asked fishermen and a despised tax collector. Jesus purposely chose men who weren't religious professionals. They weren't born charismatic leaders; none of them had seminary training. Why did Jesus pick such a motley group of men to be responsible for spreading his message throughout the world?

Powering Up

I believe one of the reasons Jesus picked those men was specifically because they *lacked* natural resources. They would *have to* rely on the power of the Holy Spirit. What else could they fall back on? When they stood up to proclaim the good news of Jesus, who else could make them effective in turning people to God? Yet when speaking about Christ, the apostles and early disciples displayed a spiritual power totally unknown in the history of world religions. "It was revealed to them that they were not serving themselves but you, when they spoke of the things that have now been told you by those who have preached the gospel to you *by the Holy Spirit sent from heaven*" (1 Peter 1:12, emphasis added).

Every believer is probably familiar with the important role that preaching and good teaching play in extending Christ's kingdom and helping us mature. But over the last few years, I've begun to wonder if our understanding of preaching is defined more by our life experience than by the Bible. In most churches, a minister stands before the congregation and shares a passage of Scripture, usually in a sequential, logical manner that breaks down the meaning of the passage for everyone to understand. Illustrations are often used, followed by an application of truth. If the message is Scripture based and the speaker's communication skills are of a high caliber, one would usually define that as a "fine sermon." The same can be applied to us when we share the Word one-on-one with a friend or coworker. The recommended advice is to use your head, be as persuasive as you can, and try to bring the person to a belief in Jesus.

While all of that is good, what are we going to make of the apostle Paul's description of his method of preaching? Reminding the Corinthian church of his eighteen-month ministry there, he said:

> When I came to you, I did not come with eloquence or human wisdom as I proclaimed to you the testimony about God. For I resolved to know nothing while I was with you except Jesus Christ and him crucified. I came to you in weakness with great fear and trembling. My message and my preaching were *not with wise and persuasive words*, but with a demonstration of the Spirit's *power*, so that your faith might not rest on human wisdom, but on God's power. (1 Cor. 2:1 – 5, emphasis added)

What? A speaker not depending on wise and persuasive words? Isn't that what most seminaries and books on effective preaching almost exclusively emphasize? Isn't that what most of us aim for when we share with others? But here the apostle states unequivocally that his message and preaching were not "with wise and persuasive words." That was never part of Paul's strategy as a preacher of the gospel. What he did claim was that his ministry involved "a demonstration of the Spirit's power"!

What kind of Spirit-saturated messages did Paul give the people in Corinth? He certainly didn't mean that every five minutes or so he interrupted his talk to heal someone's blind eyes or have the lame walk, because there is no record of that in Scripture. Yet this brilliant Pharisee-trained convert to Jesus dismisses "wise and persuasive words" and instead boasts in the Spirit's power resting on him. Why? In order that the Christians in Corinth might have their faith "in God's power" and not "human wisdom." I wonder how many of us ministers have that as our goal every time we open God's Holy Word.

Power for a Purpose

And here is some great news. There is no place in Scripture where God says that kind of help is not available to us two thousand years later. Of course, if we don't believe in that sort of supernatural anointing and Holy Spirit manifestation, we will never experience it. One of the basic principles that Jesus laid down was that according to our faith, so it will be done to us (Matt. 9:29). Unfortunately, our traditions and denominational positions on the Holy Spirit often rob us of expecting strong divine influences when we speak for Christ. May we be granted new faith in God the Spirit!

Beyond a lack of faith, there is another reason why the Holy Spirit's manifestation of power is often withheld from our lives and churches. In the beginning of Jesus' public ministry, a remarkable thing happened in the synagogue in his hometown of Nazareth. Acting as the designated reader of the Old Testament passage for that Sabbath day, the Lord read these words:

> The Spirit of the Lord is on me,
>> because he has anointed me
>> to proclaim good news to the poor.
> He has sent me to proclaim freedom for the prisoners
>> and recovery of sight for the blind,
> to set the oppressed free,
>> to proclaim the year of the Lord's favor.

Luke 4:18 – 19

Jesus then followed his public reading by these astounding words: "Today this scripture is fulfilled in your hearing" (Luke 4:21). This famous passage from Isaiah 61 was spoken of the Messiah for whom Israel was waiting. Jesus declared himself to be that Promised One. By this he explained to his own townspeople that he was much more than the mere carpenter's son they thought him to be.

Carefully note why Jesus was anointed by God and why the Spirit rested on him in power. His purpose was to bring good news to poor people with little earthly hope, to proclaim spiritual freedom to those bound by sin and Satan, to deliver the message of salvation that God wanted everyone to hear and experience. That's *why* the Holy Spirit empowered Christ so amazingly — to help sinful, needy people find their way back to God. And that's why the ascended Christ sent the Holy Spirit to the waiting disciples in the upper room. He wasn't given so we Christians could have exciting meetings as we circle the wagons and talk to one another. He wasn't promised to us for moments of spiritual ecstasy, as wonderful as that might be.

> Whenever we reach out to share the good news, we can prayerfully expect the Holy Spirit to work in power.

The Holy Spirit was sent to accomplish many divine purposes, but at the top of the list was the empowering of God's people to reach the world with the gospel of Christ. Notice Christ's words: "But you will receive power when the Holy Spirit comes on you; and *you will be my witnesses* in Jerusalem, and in all Judea and Samaria, and to the ends of the earth" (Acts 1:8, emphasis added).

If we lose sight of God's heart of love for the world — including our own cities and neighborhoods — we will experience little of the Spirit's power, since we are on a different page than our Lord is on. But whenever we reach out with purpose to share the good news of salvation through Christ; whenever we are determined to help the spiritually blind see and to set the oppressed free, we can prayerfully expect the Holy Spirit to work in power as promised by Jesus.

The Body and the Spirit

Sadly, many of us don't experience the power of the Holy Spirit because we so seldom do what Christ commissioned us to do. No matter how spiritually dark the world seems, no matter how bound and oppressed by Satan, he that is within us is greater than he that is in the world! Oh that the church of Christ would rise to its calling to be the *body of Christ* continuing his work today of reaching out in love to people who need the Lord.

Think about the needs of the people around us. We don't have to have all the answers. We don't have to know beforehand the right things to say. And more important, we should not be afraid to get down in the trenches with hurting people and their tangled lives. The Spirit's power was promised for those very situations. The Holy Spirit was sent so that all of us — whether or not we're in formal ministry — could reach out to humanity and rely on a power beyond ourselves.

Amazing "coincidences" seem to happen when we have an open heart of love and dare to reach out in Christ's name. Remember that abused fourteen-year-old girl who was so frightened of the future while she and her mother were living in a shelter? They continued to visit our church each Sunday, and there they found a new loving family of believers who ministered to them. Despite her situation, the girl was an honors student; and a few weeks later, another visitor from out of state came to our church and happened to meet her. She was a university professional, and when the woman learned about the girl's story, she huddled with her for a few moments and talked about the young lady's life. The educator's heart was moved by God's Spirit. A few minutes later she told the teenager's mom, "Don't worry. When she graduates, I am going to find a way for her to attend my university. We'll get her a scholarship by the grace of God. Just wait and see what God will do with her life."

I was present when these words were spoken. And I can still see the happy excitement and new hope dawning on the faces of both mom and daughter.

Isn't it amazing to see the Spirit work through ordinary people in extraordinary ways? How broad and beautiful life becomes when the Holy Spirit empowers us to pray, respond, counsel, listen, speak, and even awaken in the middle of the night to pray for others. Like the disciples, we are flawed people. But Jesus promised the Holy Spirit to empower us in amazing ways as we do his work on earth. Remember again the promise we looked at earlier. "If you then, though you are evil, know how to give good gifts to your children, how much more will your Father in heaven give the Holy Spirit to those who ask him!" (Luke 11:13).

All the power we need is there for the asking.

Chapter 12

THE POWER OF LOVE: DIANA'S STORY

Size is the thing that most people notice about Diana Berrios. She's so tiny! The first time I saw her, she seemed the height of a child. But it wasn't her size that caught me by surprise — it was her strength. Diana demonstrated a power beyond her human ability; in this case, it wasn't the power of the Holy Spirit. But that's getting ahead of the story.

The only reason Diana was in our church the night she first came was because someone cared about her when she was the hardest to love. As I mentioned in the preceding chapter, the Spirit moves when we're willing to reach out no matter how messy or impossible the situation seems. Someone had a God-given burden for this little fireball of a lady. And the Lord honored that faith and made Diana a remarkable trophy of God's grace.

DIANA

I tell people that I am four foot eleven, but that's a little white lie. I'm actually four foot ten. I've always been small, but so was my mother; maybe that's why it was so easy for my dad to beat her. My dad was an alcoholic, and when he got drunk, he would hit my mom. Sometimes he would grab her by the hair and throw her against the wall;

times he would take a pistol and hold it to her head. We never knew if it was loaded. It didn't matter; the fear was the same. I grew up in Spanish Harlem the third of five children. I had three sisters and a brother, and none of us could predict what would send my father into a rage.

Cops were always at our house. Sometimes my mom would try to get away. We would run to my aunt's house or my uncle's house and stay there a few days hoping he would cool down. But we always went back, and he'd continue to beat her, often really badly. It was hard to watch, and it went on for years — the whole time I was growing up. My dad would also beat my brother and sisters. But he never touched me. I don't know why. Though I was never hurt physically, the emotional damage was enormous. Sometimes I thought it would have been easier to be the one hit than to watch the people I loved get hurt.

My sisters grew up and got married just so they could get out of the house. By the time I was thirteen, I was angry and rebellious. But the only place I could go was to the streets. I started hanging with some really tough girls, girls that I could relate to. They all had the same kinds of things going on in their homes — somebody was drinking or abusive — or they came from a broken home. We could relate because we were all angry and wanting to get even with the world. So we formed our own little clique, and that became my family.

That's what I wanted — to hang out with the toughest girls. We fought, cursed, and intimidated people. Even teachers were afraid of us. But we got a lot of respect. After we got together, more people joined. We fought anyone and everyone. Eventually one of the older girls wanted to form a gang, so she named us Satan's Spades.

Soon our reputation was so well known that we actually recruited guys from the high school to join us. That was in the mid-seventies — guys usually didn't give girls that much respect — but we were so tough that even the older boys wanted to be a part of our gang. Then those guys started recruiting other guys, and we became so big we had to divide ourselves into divisions. We had three divisions, and eventually we took over a playground on 118th Street. That became our territory, and we would defend it to the death.

When other gangs tried to come into our territory, we would fight them. So I fought every day. I learned to hide blades in my rolled hair, and I greased my face so that when the other girls tried to scratch me, they couldn't get traction. Although I was small, I could fight.

But I was also out of control. Mom was so worried that she had teachers, counselors, and a couple of psychiatrists talk to me, but it didn't change anything. At school I was always in trouble. I was moved from school to school before I eventually got kicked out altogether.

That was fine with me. I stayed in the park to fight. And I did it all — smoked pot, popped pills, and sniffed glue. I was always wasted, and I didn't care how much money I needed to spend to get that way. If you put it in a bag, I would sniff it. That was who I had become. I'd often come home high, with a black eye, and argue with Mom. By then my father had moved out, but the damage was done. Mom would see evidence of the violence I was involved in, and she wouldn't know what to do.

"You're just like your dad!" she'd tell me in Spanish. "*Hija del Diablo!* You're the daughter of the devil."

Mom was a brave woman.... She wasn't afraid to come looking for me if she heard there was trouble.

We were both angry at each other. I blamed her for not standing up for her children and, most of all, for herself. She blamed me for getting messed up in the streets and turning violent like my dad.

But Mom was a brave woman. Though she was short like me, she wasn't afraid to come looking for me if she heard there was trouble. She was the only mother who dared to knock on our clubhouse door, and even during a shootout she'd come looking for me if she thought I was in trouble. She wasn't allowed in the clubhouse, but that didn't stop her. Though there were bullets flying and cops all over the place, she would still look for me, and if she found me, she'd try to drag me home.

I would grab her and say, "You got to get out of here. You got to go home. You can't be here!"

But she wasn't scared. "What bullet would want to hurt me?" she asked. She was willing to do whatever it took to get me off the streets.

One day she went to family court and got a warrant for my arrest. I was hanging out at a friend's house, and my mother figured out where I would be. She called the cops, gave them the warrant, and had me arrested. As they put me in the car, I cursed and yelled at her because I was so angry. "How could you do this to me?" I screamed. "You're my mother!" Even with all my gang activity, I had never been arrested, never been busted for anything. Now my own mom was the one who had called the cops! They sent me to a juvenile detention home in the Bronx, where I stayed for six months. When I got out, I went right back to the streets.

My mother sought help wherever she could. Her best friend was into Santeria, which is a satanic Latino religion involving voodoo, séances, mediums, and fortune-telling. Her friend had known me since I was a little girl. She told my mom to buy certain oils and plants, and then to give me a spiritual bath. The friend promised my mother that it would change my life. My mother was desperate, so she bought candles and statues of saints; some of them were really big. She made an altar in her room and put the oils and candles on the altar along with the statues. At the time, I didn't think much about it because my mother was supposed to be Catholic; and many Catholics kept statues around the house.

But then she wanted to give me baths. In the beginning, I fought her. But she would cry, so eventually I just let her do it. I would come in at three or four in the morning, high from having been out all night, and in the morning, she'd insist on my getting into the tub. She would anoint my hair and my forehead with oil, dab plants onto my body, and repeat the prayers that her friend gave her. Sometimes the prayers were to Santa Barbara or San Lazaro — always to saints I had never heard of. The prayers were in Spanish because my mother didn't speak English. Next she would take a paper with my name on it, slip it under the statue, and light candles around it while saying more prayers.

Soon I was getting baths every day. During that time, I was mostly high out of my mind, and I didn't care about the baths as long as she was off my case. That went on for years. Even when I was out on the street, she was doing weird things at home. People would come over to our house, and she and her friend would have séance parties. I don't know what they did at the parties, because I was never involved. But my mother only got in deeper. She began offering fruits in my name as a sacrifice. I would come home at three in the morning, and apples, oranges, and bananas would be all around the statues. If an orange looked good, I would just eat it. But I started to wonder if my mom was flipping out.

As I got older, I was high more often than I wasn't. I still hung out with the gang. Things hadn't changed for me, but they had for my mother. She had another friend who was a born-again Christian, and the Christian friend witnessed to my mother. My mom started going to a Spanish Pentecostal church where she accepted Jesus Christ as her Savior. She started praying for me every night. She would tell me about church and what she was learning, but I didn't want to know anything about this Jesus she kept talking about.

Over the next few months, she threw away all of the statues. One day I came in and saw her hammering a statue into small pieces and saying, "In the name of Jesus." Another day her church came over and anointed our house. *This time my mom was really flipping out.*

She would try to get me to go to church with her, but I usually refused. It was like something inside of me, something dark and spiritual, wouldn't let me go. My mother kept witnessing to me, and a few times I did go to church with her, but whenever there was an invitation to accept Christ as my Savior, I would leave. I couldn't connect with this Jesus.

It was like something inside of me, something dark and spiritual, wouldn't let me go.

In the meantime, my life got worse. Much worse. I was angry a lot. Eventually the anger took over. I no longer wanted to just fight in the gang. I wanted to hurt people. I wanted to see blood. I wanted to kill. Eventually I wanted to kill everybody. It was just a matter of time it seemed before I exploded in a murderous rage.

I felt as if something had taken control of me, as if I wasn't me anymore. Sometimes I would get into violent fits where I tried to break everything in our house. While I never touched my mother, I picked up lamps and smashed them on the floor and tore things off of the walls. I shattered things, threw things, and broke things with my bare hands. I blamed my uncontrollable rage on the drugs and the gangs, but it was more like some kind of power, a darkness, had surrounded me. I didn't know what it was or what it was doing to me.

Because of my gang connections, most people knew me in the schools, in the projects, and in the Bronx. So when my mother heard about a girl my age named Annie who had gotten saved, she figured Annie might know me. And so Mom called Annie, begging her for help. Annie had done drugs before she found Jesus, so she was familiar with me and my lifestyle. She heard my mom's desperation, and she started calling, and we'd talk.

Annie would witness to me, telling me about Jesus and inviting me to come to her church, the Brooklyn Tabernacle.

"No, I'm not going to your church," I told Annie.

But she was persistent. "Your mom's calling me every day," she said. "Every day! And she's crying, saying she doesn't know what to do with you. Let my church pray for you. Let my pastor speak to you."

I would promise to go with her, but when the time came, I would disappear and she wouldn't be able to find me. That went on for months. But despite my lies, Annie was a good friend to me, and I started telling her about the things that were happening inside of me.

One day I called her up when I was high and said, "Annie, I'm feeling like something is coming into me."

"What do you mean coming into you?"

"Like something evil is inside of me. I'm freaking out. It's the drugs I think."

"Come to church with me this Tuesday."

"Yeah, I'll go with you."

But again, when Tuesday came, I hit the streets and got high instead. Something was trying to overpower me that afternoon, so I took as many drugs as I could get my hands on. Some I didn't even know the names of — drugs I'd never even seen in all my years of getting high. Then, that evening, as I was crossing the street, a car pulled up and Annie jumped out.

"You're coming to church with me!" she said.

We started to have a battle right there on the street.

"I'm not coming to church with you!" I told her as she dragged me toward the car. "I'm not going!" I tried to fight her, but I was so blasted, I couldn't stop her.

"Come on! Just go to church with me. You said you would."

"Look, I'm going to get high. I'll come to church some other time," I said, still struggling to get away from her. "I'm leaving right now to go get high."

"If you come to church with me right now, I'll give you money."

"You're going to give me money?"

"Only if you go to church with me."

"If I go to church, you'll give me money? Really?"

"Yes, and you can do whatever you want afterward. But come with me to church."

By now I was already halfway to the car, and I knew that if Annie gave me money, I could use it to get high, so I went ahead and got in the car. Although I wanted the money, I continued to fight with her the whole way there.

Once we got to the church, she led me to some seats down near the front.

"I want my money," I said before the service started.

"After church," Annie said.

"I'm going to leave early."

"You don't get your money until the end."

I pointed to the pastor up front (Pastor Cymbala, I later learned). "See that pastor?" I said. "I don't want him to pray for me. I am just going to sit here."

The service began. There was some singing, and then the pastor spoke. Annie sang in the choir on Sundays, and although I didn't know it at the time, she had already let people in the choir know she was bringing me, and someone from the choir had alerted the pastor.

The pastor said he knew a young lady had been brought to church that night who needed Jesus really badly. He wanted Annie to bring her up so the whole church could pray for her.

"I'm not going," I told Annie. "He can pray for me while I sit right here."

But somehow, Annie got me to walk down the aisle with her. As I walked, I heard voices in my head saying they weren't going to let go of me. That I belonged to them. Then I heard a woman from the congregation say the name Jesus as part of a prayer, and all of a sudden I found myself grabbing the pastor and attacking him. I grabbed him by the throat and pushed him backwards against the platform he had been standing in front of. I spit in his face. Twice. I went crazy. A battle raged — I could hear the voices in my head as well as the people praying in the church.

Although the pastor was at least twice my size, he struggled to break free from my attack. Finally, he threw me off, and as I fell to the ground, I grabbed his shirt collar and tore it off like a piece of tissue paper. I don't remember what happened next — I was no longer in control of my body — but dozens of witnesses have told me. While I was on the floor, voices came out of my mouth, but none of them were my voice. It was as if they came from somewhere deep inside of me. They screamed, "Leave her alone! Leave her alone! She's ours, and you'll never have her! Never!"

The voices kept screaming as the pastor leaned over me. My eyes rolled up inside my head like something you'd see in a horror movie. The pastor told the evil spirits to be quiet and demanded in the name of Christ that they come out of me.

Then it was over. Whatever had control of me was gone. The evil spirits had fled. I slowly stood up, sobbing. Pastor Cymbala held up both my hands as the congregation sang a song about the blood of Jesus Christ.

That was the night I got delivered. I knew I had been set free. It was as if I had been cleansed. A peace came over me that I had never felt before. That's when I realized that I had been demon possessed and Jesus had run the evil spirits away.

That night, and for the next several nights, I stayed with people from the church. It was so awesome that those people took me into their house so I wouldn't have to go back to my old neighborhood. I felt so loved. I could hardly accept it. My language was hate, violence, and hurting. It wasn't easy for me to accept the love that came from the church and its members.

> **I knew I had been set free. A peace came over me that I had never felt before.**

The next day I called my mom. Annie had already told her what happened the night before. My mother came to visit me, and she hugged me. "I am so happy, Diana! I prayed and prayed and prayed! I didn't know what was happening to you."

Eventually I left for a treatment program. But already my life had been totally changed. I was a brand-new person. I was full of God's light and love. I began to seek him and wanted to know more about him.

I had always run with a tough gang, but that night at church was the biggest battle of my life. I think the devil knew that his time was up. He knew that he was going to be defeated and that I would be delivered from his control. That Tuesday I was delivered from more than demons. I was also delivered from drugs, anger, hatred, prejudice, and rebellion. In one second, Jesus declared, "This is where it stops." I have been walking with the Lord ever since, and not once have I ever turned back. I've never gotten high since that night. Though I still make mistakes and I sometimes get discouraged or lonely, now I can run to the Perfect One.

The devil is a liar. He never stops trying to steal, destroy, and kill. But I believe the Holy Spirit orchestrated things that night to bring me to the Brooklyn Tabernacle. People prayed for me. And people like Mom, Annie, and Pastor Cymbala weren't afraid to fight for me and to love me even when it was difficult. Through the power of the Holy Spirit, my life was forever changed.

In the end, the victory belongs to Jesus Christ.

Part Three

WHEN WE SURRENDER TO THE HOLY SPIRIT

Chapter 13

WE LOVE THE UNLOVABLE

When babies are born, the hospital staff immediately checks for certain vital signs. Is the baby breathing? Crying? Is the cry healthy or weak sounding? How much does the baby weigh? Just as breathing, crying, and size are all indicators of a newborn's physical health, there are spiritual vital signs that can tell us how healthy we are. And the most vital sign of all is love.

When we become born-again believers in Jesus Christ, we receive the new heart and spirit promised to us in the new covenant (Ezek. 11). This is nothing less than the Spirit of Christ dwelling in us. Without him, there is no true Christian experience. "If anyone does not have the Spirit of Christ, they do not belong to Christ" (Rom. 8:9). Since the Holy Spirit in us is God, and since God is love, then the essence of the one dwelling within us is divine love. No wonder Jesus said, "By this everyone will know that you are my disciples, if you love one another" (John 13:35). God's purpose for giving us his Spirit was to make that life of love possible.

Love Plays No Favorites

When the apostle Paul wrote to the church in Colosse, he told them how he thanked God when he learned of "the love you have for all God's people" (Col. 1:4). Notice the spiritual health of that congregation. It wasn't measured in attendance figures or magnificent buildings but in what really counts before God — love. And it wasn't just love for some people who were easily lovable or with the same ethnic background. No, he rejoiced in their reputation for loving all the people of God. What a great reputation to have before an unbelieving world!

Instead of a color-blind love like God's, culture, ethnicity, and race dominate the atmosphere of too much of our church life. Some groups just know they're not especially welcomed in some churches — it would be better if they stayed with their "own kind." Others have experienced churches where anger and resentment roil beneath the surface. It seems as if many congregations build walls to keep out anyone not like them instead of welcoming their brothers and sisters — like Jesus did — in love. We like to talk about love, but it's seldom the divine kind that encompasses "all the saints."

Once while I was overseas, a friend of mine arranged a meeting with a small group of Christian businessmen. He wanted me to share a specific financial challenge our church was facing in downtown Brooklyn with hopes that these men might be able to help us. When I completed my short, informal presentation, they quite frankly laid out their position. Although blessed with great financial resources, and although extreme poverty rarely exists in their country, they said they only helped "their own kind." The thought of reaching out in love to people who were not like them seemed unthinkable.

Too often, isn't that our subconscious frame of reference? If the people are "different" — meaning not our color or ethnicity, or not a part of our congregation or denomination — their plight in life rarely touches our hearts. But God's love knows no such parameters. It's free flowing and as wide as the world. It recognizes no outward distinction and overflows every human wall of separation. It's the love of God, his very essence. God sent Jesus into a world that was as much different or "other" to his holy nature as one could imagine. But divine love has only one target group — the entire human race! God's love plays no favorites. His followers on earth were given the Holy Spirit so we could "be imitators of God … and *live a life of love*, just as Christ loved us and gave himself up for us as a fragrant offering and sacrifice to God" (Eph. 5:1 – 2, emphasis added).[1]

Love Like a Nursing Mother

Earlier I mentioned that morning in a London hotel room when God made some passages in 1 Thessalonians come alive to me. Like most ministers, I had studied the apostle Paul in hopes of gleaning the secrets of such powerfully effective labor for Christ. I already knew his unchanging message — the gospel of Jesus Christ. I had also analyzed his methodology: he depended totally on the Holy Spirit. Daily he was led and strengthened by the Spirit's power.

But now a third truth began to jump off the pages of my New Testament — Paul's motivation. In reminding the believers of his visit to Thessalonica, which resulted in their conversions and the founding of a Christian church, Paul said, "As apostles of Christ we could have been a burden to you, but we were gentle among you, like a mother caring for her little children" (1 Thess. 2:6 – 7).[2] The picture here in the original Greek is of a mother pulling down the bodice of her dress and nursing the baby at her breast. What a tender picture of love and devotion. When a mother nurses an infant, it's all about the baby, not her. Paul declared that was how he was while among them — all the attention and concern was for them, not him. The apostle's motivation was a fervent love for the believers in Thessalonica that could only be explained by God's own love controlling him.

But then he went further: "We loved you so much that we were delighted to share with you not only the gospel of God but our lives as well, because you had become so dear to us" (1 Thess. 2:8).[3] We loved you so much, Paul said, that we didn't want to share only the gospel with you, but *our own lives* as well! No wonder his messages reached the hearts of the people. His words were not only from his mouth, but also from a tender heart. What would make a minister want to give not just sermons to people, but his very life as well? It was love. He was willing to sacrifice his life because these people had become so dear to him that no cost or sacrifice would be too much. We see here a man motivated by the strongest force in the universe — God's love replicated in and through him.

> We see in Paul a man motivated by the strongest force in the universe — God's love replicated in and through him.

I wept as I sat on the floor with my New Testament in my lap. How short I had fallen from that kind of ministry. I was too self-absorbed and self-conscious to let go and let God's love flow through me. In my insecurity, I was too often just trying to get through the sermon without fumbling and hoped that possibly someone might comment favorably. Like a mother nursing her baby? Ready to give my life for the sheep? No way. I saw my mechanical, unloving efforts in God's clear light, and it kept me before Him in prayer for a long time. I didn't need my batteries recharged; I needed a spiritual overhaul, a new way of living.

My prayer since then has repeatedly been that God would enable me to see people the way he sees them and to feel what he feels no matter what. Though I have failed countless times, that remains my constant petition at the throne of grace.

A Life Worthy of Love

That kind of love is not reserved for a few select believers or special men and women involved in ministry. It's what Paul calls "a life worthy of the Lord" (Col. 1:10), and it's God's purpose for every one of us. Now that his love has provided our salvation, how unworthy of him are lives lived in selfishness, bickering, and prejudice. And after all of his mercy, how can we be judgmental with other people? Is that our experience with Jesus? Has he jumped down our throats when we failed? Has he put us on some losers' list because of our inconsistencies and broken promises? No, his love endures and has proved greater than all our faults.

A life of love is also the only way to "please him in every way" (Col. 1:10). Since God is an emotional being, he experiences joy and sadness just as we do. Our daily words and deeds can cause him displeasure or move him to rejoice over us with singing. What an amazing thought! Today you and I can please the God of the universe. Although he is beyond our comprehension, omnipotent, omnipresent, and omniscient, his heart can still be touched by our loving actions, even in commonplace activities. What else but love could please a God of love?

Love is always the bottom line. That's why the Bible declares: "For in Christ Jesus neither circumcision nor uncircumcision has any value. The only thing that counts is faith expressing itself through love" (Gal. 5:6). Even though the sign of God's covenant with Abraham was the circumcision of all baby boys, a new day has dawned and a better covenant has been established. Circumcision, race, talent, money, fame, education, or anything else we highly treasure becomes irrelevant in comparison with love. Each of us individually and every Christian church has been ordained by God to reveal this love as the indisputable sign that we belong to Christ.

The Power of Love

A loving person, or better yet, a church full of loving people, has tremendous power to influence people for God. A few years ago, an older couple from a southern state visited our church. We had a mutual friend, and the couple came to my office after the service so we could be introduced. They both seemed a little emotional as we chatted, and soon I learned why.

"Pastor," the man said, "I want to tell you something before we leave. We go to a very conservative church, and the service we were just in was very different for us. But it was more than the loud singing, hands lifted, and the obvious emotion of your congregation. We understand that, and we were blessed by it all. But you see"— he paused, his voice cracking— "we've never worshiped with black people and Latinos before, never once in our lives." Then he continued. "What's more, when you directed folks to greet one another, all kinds of men I've never met hugged me as if I was their brother." Tears now filled his eyes. "I felt more love this morning from strangers than I've ever experienced in my home church for the past thirty years."

What a blessing! He never mentioned my sermon or how the choir sang. What touched his heart and opened his eyes was God's love flowing beyond all the fences that had been carefully (and religiously) erected over the decades of his life. The love he experienced that day wasn't something that could be taught to a congregation. "Now about your love for one another we do not need to write to you, for you yourselves have been taught by God to love each other" (1 Thess. 4:9). God is the instructor and dean of students in the school of love. For us he makes the lesson amazingly clear: "God is love. Whoever lives in love lives in God, and God in them" (1 John 4:16). There it is for all of us to ponder.

"Whoever lives in love"—that's the final exam for each of us.

Doctrinal *discussions* (not fights) have their place. But it's not our Calvinism, Pentecostalism, evangelicalism, or any other "ism" that proves we live in God. It's only love. It often seems to me that the so-called culture wars that take place in the name of God and morality can often radiate more bitterness than love. That defeats the purpose of Jesus' message. "Love does no harm to a neighbor. Therefore love is the fulfillment of the law" (Rom. 13:10). Of course, we're not the first to need an attitude correction. When Paul wrote to the Corinthians about whether they could eat food that was sacrificed to idols, he started his answer by addressing the tone of the conversation. "We know that 'We all possess knowledge.' But knowledge puffs up while love builds up" (1 Cor. 8:1).

Nothing is accomplished when we fuss with others in an unloving way. The outside world looks in and says, "If that's the way Christians are, I don't want any part of it!" If we want Christianity to be attractive to unbelievers, we need to represent ourselves in a loving way. Jesus was a friend to sinners. It is love that drew people to him. They liked to hang out with him. I wonder how many unbelievers could say the same about us. "Whoever lives in love" — that's the final exam for each of us. May God help us to remember it always.

Love in the Spirit

Perhaps the hardest question we need to address is, how did those believers in Colosse develop that strong love for all the saints? How did Paul get to the place of unselfishly caring for people like a nursing mother, willing to make any sacrifice, if necessary, for their spiritual welfare? Paul gives us the answer when he explains that another minister told him about "your *love in the Spirit*." It wasn't an earth-based love that the saints in Colosse were experiencing; it was the Holy Spirit's love replacing their human limitations and carnal tendencies. It was supernatural love because it belonged to God — God, the Holy Spirit.

This is an important lesson for us. Most of us know that Christ is the perfect model of love. We know the message in 1 Corinthians 13 about the preeminence of love, and we know that God is love. But then we foolishly try harder, to love more, in our own strength. We make well-meaning deliberate attempts to overcome selfish habits and our natural distaste for cranky, obnoxious people. But when we react unkindly and sense failure, we just go back to the drawing board, convinced that if we only try harder, or read more Scriptures, we'll somehow get better at loving others.

But Paul spoke of "love in the Spirit," which is something totally separate from human ability. Remember his teaching to the Galatians: "The fruit of the Spirit is love" (Gal. 5:22). Love is a fruit growing within us from a supernatural source. It's not your love, yet it is, since the Spirit works in you both to will and to do loving things that are on his mind. You never hear of an apple tree struggling to produce its fruit. As long as sap flows within the tree, apples will form and blossom. And so it is with the Holy Spirit and love. He is our life and bears the fruit — not us. That's why he was sent to live in us.

How else could Stephen, as he was being stoned, say, "Lord, do not hold this sin against them" (Acts 7:60)? What else could make Paul compare his love for the Thessalonians to a nursing mother and her baby? Or say that he was ready to give up his life for them? Only the love of God could make them love like that.

Without the miracle of God's love, life has a way of hardening all of us. We become cynical, crusty senior citizens without the glow of the "first love" we experienced at the beginning of our life in Christ. This is not only bad for us but also for the cause of Christ to a watching world. But it doesn't have to be that way: "They will still bear fruit in old age, they will stay fresh and green" (Ps. 92:14).

Let's ask for a fresh baptism of God's love. Let's then walk in that love so everyone encountering us can have a peek into the heart of God.

Chapter 14

WE ARE DRAWN INTO FELLOWSHIP

Have you ever met a father who is no longer speaking to his son? Perhaps they were close while the son was growing up, but they had an argument, words were said, and they haven't spoken since. Maybe you know a woman who doesn't get along with her sister. Conversations between them are few and strained. Perhaps there is a couple in your social circle who, although they are married and still live together, don't communicate and don't enjoy each other's company.

Those individuals have a relationship, and they even have the legal documents — a birth certificate or a marriage license — to prove it. But do they have *fellowship* with each other? How can a relationship be significant if there isn't at least a sense of camaraderie or intimacy between the parties?

As Christians we have a relationship with God. He is our Father and we are his children. But just because we have a relationship doesn't mean that we necessarily have the kind of fellowship God planned for us.

The Importance of Fellowship

When we read the writings of some of the great Christian leaders from a hundred years ago or earlier, we see that there was a strong emphasis on two-way fellowship between the Lord and his people. They wrote about not just spending time praising and thanking God, or even petitioning him, but also about spending time just waiting in his presence and listening for his voice. Fellowship with God is more than just attending church on Sunday; it is about spending time alone with God.

We have no better model for this than Jesus, who "often withdrew to lonely places and prayed" (Luke 5:16). Although the Son of God, Jesus found it necessary to spend time alone with God in prayer, to discern what God wanted him to do. How else would he know how long to stay in Capernaum or Jerusalem unless he heard it from God? Jesus certainly did not talk and petition God during all those hours he was away by himself. Instead, he listened to his Father for guidance and for the very subject matter of his teaching: "These words you hear are not my own; they belong to the Father who sent me" (John 14:24).

It was while communing with the Father that Jesus was directed to pick twelve men to be his followers. "Jesus went up on a mountainside and called to him those he wanted, and they came to him. He appointed twelve that they might be with him and that he might send them out to preach and to have authority to drive out demons" (Mark 3:13 – 15). It's interesting to note the first reason Mark gives for appointing the Twelve. *That they might be with him.* When Jesus called someone, fellowship came before ministry.

Unlike the apostles, however, we can't hang out with Jesus on the mountainside or get together to go fishing. For us, that fellowship can only happen through the person of the Holy Spirit.

In Ephesians, Paul says that through Jesus, both Jews and Gentiles "have access to the Father by one Spirit" (2:18). In other words, because of Jesus' sacrifice on the cross, we now have the Spirit who brings us into God's presence. The active work of the Holy Spirit makes fellowship with God a real and rich experience that brings strength to our souls.

My worst days in life didn't happen because I lost my relationship with God, but because I had no time for fellowship — fellowship through the Word, fellowship in prayer, in waiting on God, in talking to God, in listening to God. When we run around so much, we're weakened; we have less faith, we have less grace, and we have more stress. There is something about being with Jesus, being in God's presence, that helps us have more peace and joy.

He Wakens My Ear to Listen

When we spend time with God, we should want to do more than just present a list of requests — we need to listen for his voice. Someone once said, "What's more important? Us telling God our requests, which he already knows before we tell him, or us listening for his voice, to hear what is on *his* heart?"

I know some people don't believe we can still hear God's voice. "He has already said what he is going to say in the Bible." They would argue that hearing from God is religious fanaticism or a form of scary emotionalism. But the history of the Christian church totally negates that belief. How else would people like British missionary Hudson Taylor — who, while spending time with the Lord, felt God put a call on his heart to go to China — have brought the gospel to unreached people in Asia? In fact, how would any missionary who has ever done something great for God have known to do it unless God had first communicated it to them? There is no verse in the Bible that says, "Go to Bangladesh!"

Although we all know that the Bible is complete, God does still speak.

Although we all know that the Bible is complete and God does not speak to replace doctrine or communicate on the same level of Scripture, he does still speak. He might offer vital words of warning or convicting messages that have personal application. Sometimes it is a word of guidance — a direction we should move in. That kind of direction is heard only by a listening ear and a hearing heart.

One of my favorite passages is found in Isaiah.

> The Sovereign LORD has given me a well-instructed tongue,
>   to know the word that sustains the weary.
> He wakens me morning by morning,
>   *wakens my ear to listen* like one being instructed.
>   *Isaiah 50:4, emphasis added*

Isaiah was saying that it was the Lord who taught him what to say, especially words that would sustain the weary. But that only happened because in the morning his spiritual ears were awakened to listen. Although Isaiah described his own experience, history has proven that housewives, school teachers, and truck drivers — in fact, anyone who belongs to the Lord — can enjoy the blessing of this kind of fellowship with a listening ear.

When another prophet, Samuel, was a young boy, he thought he heard his teacher Eli calling his name. It was actually the Lord, but Samuel didn't yet know the Lord's voice. After Samuel inquired of Eli three times, Eli instructed Samuel to say, "Speak, Lord, for your servant is listening." Later all of Israel flocked to Samuel to hear the word of the Lord that he received through fellowship with God. It was through fellowship with God that Moses received the Ten Commandments and the building plans for the tabernacle. Later, through listening, David received instructions on how to build the temple that his son Solomon would construct. God speaks to those who listen.

In the New Testament era, a simple believer named Ananias received Christ's instructions to go to the recently converted Saul of Tarsus and minister to him. He wasn't a prophet, but he heard from God a message not of new doctrine but of personal direction. Why wouldn't the Holy Spirit still want to guide the Christian believer today?

As we spend time listening to God, we can be taught what to say and be given words for that day. Sometimes we're given a general feeling or section of Scripture that prepares our heart for the things that will soon confront us. At other times, God might give us a specific verse, nugget of wisdom, or word of encouragement that we can pass on to someone we meet during the day. But this listening ear and instructed tongue come only from times of fellowship with the Lord. It comes while we're listening, not when we are talking.

A Man Who Listened

For weeks I had noticed a tall, handsome guy attending our Tuesday night prayer meetings. I had seen him around the church in passing, and I'd heard bits and pieces of his story. I knew that he traveled a great distance each day to come and volunteer at the church. But at those weekly prayer meetings, I would see him huddled in a corner of the floor, sometimes sitting against a wall, sometimes kneeling, but always waiting. Even after everyone else had drifted away, he was still there. I'd be praying with people or waiting on God myself and see this young man there but not know what was going on. By his posture and prayerful attitude, I sensed he was tender and listening. What was he listening for? What was he searching for? Then I heard his whole story and learned that this was a young man who had a listening heart.

Todd Crews grew up in a basketball-loving family from a small town in southern Indiana. During most of high school, he was more interested in partying than he was in religion, but when his mother gave her life to Jesus, it transformed the whole family. Todd became a Christian in his senior year. He knew he wanted to go to college, but two months before graduation, he still hadn't decided where. He prayed about it and felt that God was leading him to attend a Christian college. He applied and was accepted to Palm Beach Atlantic University in Florida.

As a sophomore in college, Todd visited New York City. He said, "I heard about a church, the Brooklyn Tabernacle, that had lines wrapped around the block for people to get in. I had never heard of anything like that before, so I went to check it out." While attending a service, Todd was moved by the worship, the people he met, and the love he felt. "I was overwhelmed by the presence of God, and while I was there, I just sensed God speaking to me. I didn't know that God's Spirit could move in such a way in a church. It wasn't a production. It wasn't entertainment. It was just people worshiping and hungering after more of God."

Todd spent the summer before his senior year of college praying and seeking God's will for his life. While his friends lined up jobs, Todd was unsure of what to do or where to go. "Midway through my college career, I knew that God was calling me to full-time ministry, but I didn't know in what capacity," Todd said. "I was totally open, telling God I would do whatever he wanted, go wherever he wanted me to go, or stay and work in the ministry where I was already working." Once again, two months before graduation, Todd heard from God. It was during an intense experience of seeking God's will for his life while praying and weeping on the beach that Todd heard God say, "Go to Brooklyn and serve."

"That was all," Todd said. "It was very vague, and there were no details. I couldn't help but wonder if I was the one who thought it up. I had attended the Tabernacle that one time during my visit to New York City three years earlier, and I knew they weren't the kind of church to post employment opportunities online. So I didn't tell anybody about what I had heard, and I just kept praying and asking God if this was really from him."

A few weeks later, Todd was back in Indiana attending a basketball tournament with his dad. They were just leaving when someone randomly offered them tickets for that night's Indiana Pacers' game. Tip-off was in fifteen minutes. They accepted and left for the arena. Once they found their seats, Todd struck up a conversation with the man next to him. Todd learned the man's name was Richie McKay. He was the head basketball coach at the University of

> **"I didn't tell anybody about what I had heard, and I just kept asking God if this was really from him."**

New Mexico, and he was also a Christian. During the game, they talked about a lot of things, and then at one point Richie asked Todd, "What are you going to do after you graduate?"

"Well, there's this church up in Brooklyn, and I've been thinking about going up there and seeing if I could help out in some way."

"What's the name of the church?"

"It's called the Brooklyn Tabernacle."

"Really? My good friend works there, and he's actually in Indianapolis right now. We should get you two together."

The next day, Todd met Craig Holliday, one of our staff members. "I just shared my heart with him," Todd said. "I told him that I wanted to be a part of what God was doing there, and that I would come up and literally scrub toilets if it meant I could be a part of everything."

"Great!" Craig said, handing Todd his card. "Call me when you get there."

"I knew it wasn't a job offer, but it was the confirmation I needed that this was from God and not something I made up in my head."

Back in Florida, Todd graduated, packed up his car, and drove to New York City. By then, his parents were living in West Point, in upstate New York, so he went to live with them. The day after he arrived, he called Craig, and they set up a time to meet for lunch in Brooklyn. It was a fifty-mile drive that could take two and a half hours each way. "I went to lunch with him, but there wasn't any opportunity for a job. Instead, Craig just offered to introduce me around and invited me to come to a service." Todd was disappointed, but he took Craig up on the offer and met some of the people who are a part of our church. Eventually he was offered a volunteer job in the church's Downtown Learning Center library.

"It wasn't cleaning toilets," Todd said, "but I had to put stickers on every single book in the entire library. It was a good-sized room full of books, and I was in there by myself for eight hours a day putting on stickers." But Todd used the time well. He would listen to sermons on the computer, he would pray, and he would listen to God. "I began to meet people, and they started giving me more responsibilities." Todd also began teaching classes and tutoring students in the center.

After three months of commuting two and a half hours each way for a volunteer job, Todd got discouraged. "I wondered what I was doing there and if it was ever going to evolve into something else." Around that time, my son-in-law, Pastor Brian Pettrey, heard what Todd had been doing and invited him to come live with his family. Todd refused at first, not wanting to put anyone out. But Brian wouldn't take no for an answer, and eventually Todd moved in.

"I stayed with his family for seven months," Todd said. "That turned out to be one of the best experiences of my life because it was such a learning opportunity. I got to see him be a pastor, father, and husband, and to see how a family worked with Christ at the center."

One day during that time, I called Todd into my office because I finally had an opportunity for him. I wanted him to work with my daughter Susan to reorganize BT Kids — our children's ministry. I could see the disappointment in his eyes. He told me later, "I love kids, but I didn't want to do kids' ministry. I didn't think I had the skills, and it certainly wasn't my desire to work with kids."

A few weeks later, he came back to me and asked if he could do something else. But we didn't have any other opportunities available, and I could already see the impact he was making, so I asked him to stick with it. Todd kept seeking the Lord and listening for his voice. Again, through waiting and listening, Todd heard God speak. "I felt like he told me that I should do it as long as it took, because that would make me more like him." But something else happened along the way; God gave Todd a heart for kids. "I started to pour my life into it, and I got really passionate about the kids."

During the next few months, Todd also volunteered in the young adult ministry. "I really had a passion for that." Later when the pastor who was leading that ministry left, I asked Todd to take over the leadership. "It really surprised me," Todd said. "It is for nineteento thirty-year-olds, and at the time, I was only twenty-three. I was young and inexperienced, but I loved serving them."

Todd had prayed, waited, and listened for a long time before he found God's niche for him. But it was because he listened and obeyed that it all came to fruition. "There were so many times I was discouraged, but God would just impress on me to stay put. 'This is where I want you, and don't worry, it will all fall into place.'" Now Todd would tell you that those waiting experiences, while hard at the time, were some of the most precious experiences he has ever had. "When I was teaching those classes, I met a lot of great people. The five-hour daily drives gave me time to process those meetings, to pray for people, and to weep for the things they went through."

> The Spirit was able to do great things through him because he had a patient, teachable spirit.

As I learned more about Todd and watched his story unfold, I knew why he stayed so late in those prayer meetings. He felt his need for fellowship with God, to wait on him and listen for his still, small voice. Having served humbly and faithfully in the shadows, Todd Crews has now been elevated to a strategic leadership role in our church. The Spirit was able to do great things through him because he had a patient, teachable spirit and allowed the Lord to prepare his heart for what came next.

The Love of the Father

Martin Luther, the sixteenth-century priest who initiated the Protestant Reformation, was initially afraid of God because he believed that the Lord was a holy but angry judge. That's what the legalism of his day taught him to believe. No matter how hard Martin tried to please this holy God, he failed, felt condemned by God, and experienced the guilt of his sin. Some of us have the same battles — we're up against a god who is some sort of harsh, austere king that delights in punishing us. But that is not who God is. He is a loving Father who is full of mercy and patience. Without a proper understanding of who he is, a life of intimate fellowship is impossible.

I love spending time with my grandson Levi. I enjoy just having him on my lap and being with him. He doesn't have to do anything; I don't need him to perform or sing to give me great joy. Similarly, the Lord is that kind of Father who delights in his family. He wants us to come into his presence because he loves us and wants to spend time with his children.

In Romans 8, Paul says: "The Spirit you received does not make you slaves, so that you live in fear again; rather, the Spirit you received brought about your adoption to sonship. And by him we cry, 'Abba, Father.' The Spirit himself testifies with our spirit that we are God's children" (vv. 15–16). What an important passage that is! Paul tells us that the Spirit will bear witness to our spirit — to our innermost being — that we *are God's children* and he is *our Father*. Through the work of the Holy Spirit, we can experientially *know* that God loves us. We don't have to be afraid. He is not merely the omnipotent creator and ruler of the universe. He is also Abba, Father, the tenderest and most loving Dad anyone could have as a parent.

The Spirit assures us that God is our loving Father. He feels no anger toward us though we have sinned and failed him so many times. Our well-deserved punishment was completely borne by Jesus on the cross. There is not one blot of transgression against us in his sight. As a loving Father, he *will* discipline his children, but *not in a judicial way*. His chastening is done in love for our good that we may become like Christ in every area of our lives.

During quiet times of fellowship, the Holy Spirit makes God's love real, not just in our heads, but also in our hearts. When God's Spirit is moving, we have rest and peace. We know we don't have to strive for a personal righteousness of our own to gain acceptance before God. We are secure in what Jesus Christ did for us on the cross, and we can approach God boldly.

Broken Fellowship

There are times, though, when we get out of sync with God — when we don't have the kind of fellowship that he longs for and we need. During those moments, I am reminded of the church in Laodicea. Jesus told them, "Here I am! I stand at the door and knock. If anyone hears my voice and opens the door, I will come in and eat with that person, and they with me" (Rev. 3:20). When Jesus requested to share a meal with them, he was speaking of his desire for fellowship with the Laodicean church, but for some reason he was found standing *outside* the door seeking entrance. Imagine the tragedy of Christ locked out and separate from the believers for whom he died on the cross! What was the remedy for them and for us? Christ directed them to repent of everything that raised a wall between them and him. That would enable them to freely open their hearts to enjoy sweet communion with their Savior.

I love this brief excerpt from an old book in my library. The author describes God's desire for fellowship and how we can lose that intimacy if we allow our hearts to wander away and become cold:

> The church is the glory, crown, joy, and fullness of Christ; over it He is especially Lord; in it He delights to dwell, as in His "own house"; and when any of the living stones that compose this spiritual temple meet together in His name, thither he especially resorts — "there am I in the midst of them."
>
> But as we may individually walk so as to grieve Him, and thereby lose the sense of His presence in our souls, we may also collectively so dishonor Him, by neglecting His word, and turning aside from reliance on His Spirit, as to render our assemblies powerless and dead; the living presence of Christ may not be experienced, and fellowship with Him may altogether be lost.
>
> We may be assured of this, that if we desire to have the consciousness of the Lord's presence with us when we meet together, we must each cultivate communion with Him in our own hearts and homes — we shall find the best way to ensure a happy meeting with the saints will be to be happy with the Lord Himself in private.
>
> When, therefore, we find our little assemblies are cold and spiritless, let us ask ourselves if our own hearts have not been previously wandering away from the Lord; for if the majority of us bring cold and worldly hearts, our collective meeting will partake of the deadness of those who mainly compose it.[1]

If we desire a more intimate relationship with God, we will be encouraged to remember the story of the prodigal son. After breaking fellowship with his father and wasting money on riotous living, the son humbly returned home and asked to be a mere servant and to live in the barn. But the father would have none of that. Instead, a robe was placed on him, a ring was put on his finger, and sandals were slid on his feet. The father didn't want to dwell on the son's past mistakes; he only wanted to receive him into the house, sit him down at the banquet table, and eat with him.

That's what God's heart wants for all of us today. He sent his Son to wash away our sins, and now the Spirit has been sent to bring us the Father's invitation. "Come into the house, sit at my table, and eat with me."

Imagine sitting down to dinner with our Lord — what an intimate and glorious evening that would be! Robert Murray M'Cheyne, a minister in the Church of Scotland in the first half of the nineteenth century, said, "A calm hour with God is worth a whole lifetime with man." We don't have to imagine what that meal might be like. That kind of fellowship is available to us at any moment of any day through the Spirit. We only need to ask.

Chapter 15

A FEARFUL LIFE AND A CRY FOR FELLOWSHIP: TERRY'S STORY

Terry Khem had the misfortune of being born in Cambodia in the early 1970s, just as the Khmer Rouge regime was getting under way and killing large numbers of people, as portrayed in the film *The Killing Fields*. I want to warn you that parts of her story are incredibly hard to read; I can only imagine how hard they were to live through. During even the most trying times of her life, Terry longed to be loved by a father, but because her environment was so poisoned by the atrocities around her, she never found that kind of love. Yet the Spirit continued to draw her to the light, despite her own protestations, until she experienced a new life in Christ and the acceptance she always craved. Remarkably, Terry has been able to forgive the atrocities committed against her, and through the power of the Spirit, she has overcome her fears. Today she desires to use the love and fellowship she has found in Christ to help others who are in similar situations.

TERRY

The war in Cambodia had only been going on for a year when my father disappeared. He got ill, and some men said they were going to take him to a hospital, but they didn't. Either they killed him, or they left him in the jungle to die. I don't know what happened, because I never saw him again. I was born sometime between 1970 and 1972. In my country, people don't know the date of their birth unless they come from a very rich family. But I do know it was 1975 when my father disappeared.

The authorities also took many of the children in our town. The men said if a child could eat, walk, and talk, they could work. One day they came through and took as many children as they could up to the mountains to a forced labor camp. Fortunately, my mother was very clever. When the military came through, she hid my little sister and I so that we wouldn't be taken.

During the day, while the adults were at work, inspectors would come through to see if anyone was hiding food. My sister and I hid in our attic. We quietly spent most of our day there. After the inspectors left, we could climb down from the attic and play. In the evenings, we were free to roam among the village, because we wouldn't be discovered when we mixed in with the other children who hadn't been taken.

Men and women were required to work from four in the morning until almost midnight. From 1975 to 1979, there wasn't one day that the people in our town got enough sleep. And there was never enough food. The workers got a big bowl of water, some rice, and a salt rock. But those who didn't work didn't get to eat. My sister and I had to wait for our mother to return home and give us her food.

In the evening after the workers returned, the authorities typically held a meeting. If, during their inspections, the officials had found that someone had stolen food, hidden gold, or disobeyed orders, they would make an example of them.

The authorities would gather everyone in the center of town, including the children, and force us to watch as they crucified people — literally nailed them to crosses. I remember watching one couple getting crucified together because they refused to marry. I was young, and it was hard to watch, but that wasn't the worst form of execution. The one that horrified me the most was when they made people dig a hole and then pushed them into it, or dumped a truckload of people into it, and then buried them alive. They would claw and scrape at the earth as they tried to save themselves from the inevitable.

We were told that we couldn't cry and that we couldn't have sympathy. If you got sick watching the torture, they killed you on the spot. If a baby cried, they would take the baby away from his or her mother. Best case, the parents would never see their child again, but worst case, the soldiers would murder the child right in front of the mother. Dead bodies were always in the streets. Death was everywhere. But we became indifferent because we were trained not to feel.

I watched other children, friends of mine, die from hunger. The girl next door chewed on herself because she was starving. She was so skinny and so hungry that she would chew on her ankle. Eventually she chewed herself to death. I watched people kill their wives and their daughters just to eat the meat. We knew our destiny was death anyway, so what did it matter if it came sooner rather than later? We never grieved the loss of a life; the only pain we felt was the pain of hunger.

We never grieved the loss of a life; the only pain we felt was the pain of hunger.

At some point, the soldiers forced us to leave our homes and live in the jungle. After three months, all the government and military officials suddenly disappeared. We returned home, but all the officials were gone from there too. We realized the war must be over. We had freedom!

But the food was gone too. If we were going to survive, we had to get to the city. People came from the city in wagons to pick up their family members and take them back. We were able to get a ride with my father's first wife. Somehow my mother had remained friendly with her even after she married my father.

The day we left our house, bodies were piled in the street. As I looked closer, I discovered some of them weren't yet dead. They were just unable to walk; they were so sick or injured they couldn't go on. As I climbed into the cart, I heard a baby. She was lying on the side of the road crying. She was so little. "Mom, can we take the baby?" I asked.

"No, honey. It's not our cart. We need to escape, and the cart is already full. Maybe the mother will come back for her baby."

As the cart pulled away, an unbelievable hatred and anger filled me as I realized how hopeless that baby's future was and how helpless I was to do anything about it. The baby continued to cry. And something inside me died. From that moment on, I stopped talking. People thought I was mute. For the next few years, I responded with only a yes, no, or okay.

When we arrived in the city, the war had been over for about three months, yet there was still no one in control. People had been taught to think so little of life that they continued to kill. The city was in complete chaos. There was no food. Women and children without a man to protect them were at the greatest risk of starving. There were a lot of single and widowed women with children; their husbands had either been killed or worked to death under the communist regime. So the remaining men went crazy. They would take four or five different wives. "If you don't marry me," they'd threaten a woman, "I will kill your children."

One day while mother was out scavenging for food, a man approached her. "Do you want food?"

"Yes!" my mom said. "I have two kids I need to feed."

"You marry me, and I will spare your life. But if you don't, I will kill you and your children."

"You don't even know where I live."

"Don't worry, I'll find out."

My mother ran from him. But later that day, he showed up where we lived. She had no choice but to "marry" him. At first my sister and I were excited. Our father had been taken away from us, and now we were going to have a dad again! Our dad had been kind and compassionate, and I always knew we were loved. I couldn't believe our good fortune! But we soon learned our new stepfather wasn't anything like our dad. He would beat my mom, sister, and me, and take whatever he could from us to satisfy his drinking. He would bring drunk men over to our house at all hours, and he also had another wife living somewhere else.

After a while, our stepfather got into trouble with the new government. They were planning to put him in jail. A few days later, I noticed my mother and stepfather packing things. Then, in the middle of the night, my mom woke us up. "We are leaving. Get your things; we must go."

We tied up the belongings we could carry and left the house. The plan was to cross the jungle to Thailand. We had heard about a Red Cross shelter for war refugees on the Thai side of the border. We didn't have shoes or warm clothes, and it was during our rainy season, so we were often soaked and cold at night. Sometimes we walked in water that was knee high; other times it was up to our necks. Then there were days when we had no food or water.

The more we walked, the more we joined with other groups, and the larger the crowds grew. It felt as if the whole country was escaping. And there were so many landmines! It seemed as if every ten minutes someone would step on one and we'd hear a loud explosion.

Sometimes I would wake up to see body parts from landmine victims littering the area. One day we were walking behind a family with a cart being pulled by a cow. Suddenly they just exploded. The cow, the cart, the people — everything exploded into the air and rained down on us in little pieces. After the explosion, I heard gunfire from the back of the line. "Shooting! They're shooting!" people shouted. Because we were in the middle, we had time to run to the bush and hide from the snipers.

Somehow we made it to the camp in Thailand. We stayed in that camp, living under a tree for three days until we were transferred to a second camp. Then again, after that place filled, we were transferred once again. At the third camp, we got a cement hut that we shared with another family. It was just one big square room built up off the ground. The ground was used for cooking.

That camp also had a school for children. It wasn't much, but they taught the Cambodian alphabet and numbers. Though I still didn't speak, by now I was twelve years old and I was desperate to learn. I wanted to be a journalist so I could expose what had gone on in my country. Hate and anger still burned inside of me, and I thought that if I could write my story, I could let generations of people know about the life we had lived.

> I thought that if I could write my story, I could let generations of people know about the life we had lived.

But my mother had another child, so I wasn't allowed to go to school. I had to stay home and help take care of the baby.

The principal of the school lived next door. He was a very educated man, and everyone looked up to him. And unlike my stepfather, he was also kind to his family. At night he would give lessons to his own children at his home. So every day, without being invited, I would go there and listen to him teach his family. He allowed me and my sister to take part in the lessons; it was the only education I got.

One night, the camp had a play, and most of the adults and children went to see it. I was home alone, and so was the principal who lived next door. I walked over to his house because I wanted to learn. He asked me, "Do you want to feel what it is like to have a father? How a father loves his daughter?"

I still wasn't speaking, so I just nodded. I was desperate to feel the love of a father.

He took me into his house. "I'll show you, but it will be our secret. It will just be between you and me."

We went inside, where he began to use me sexually. From then on, he would look for opportunities for his house to be empty. When no one was there, he would come and find me. And since I didn't speak, I didn't say anything to anyone. He knew I wouldn't. It happened so often that it became a normal part of life for me until his family got sponsored to leave the camp and move to America.

Later, as the camp neared capacity, another husband and wife moved into our hut. The house was divided by some fabric that we hung, but even then I could hear the man beating his wife. One day I was there alone, and I didn't realize the man was on the other side of the fabric. I was cleaning our side of the hut when he grabbed me and pulled me over to his side. He stuck a small piece of candy into my mouth and whispered into my ear, "If you make a noise, I will kill you." And I knew he would. I knew what was coming, and all I could think was, *Get it over with.* My nightmare of sexual abuse continued.

After he finished, I ran to the Buddhist temple they had built inside the camp. I entered the temple and approached the god, a statue of Buddha, and said, "I don't know what I have done to have a life like this." I shook my fist and continued. "I will never ever accept that there is a god in this world, and I will never submit to any god. From today forward, my life is my own, and I will take care of myself." It was the first time I had spoken words out loud in years.

I hated men. I hated my father for leaving me behind. I hated my stepfather and others who had used me. I hated life. I became calloused and cold and no longer responded with even a yes, no, or okay. My stepfather would hit me, and I would just sit there and let him do it. I wouldn't even cry, which just made him angrier. As he hit me, I let the bitterness grow.

In 1985 we moved through a series of camps, always getting closer to the population centers, until finally we were transferred to New York. I was excited to come to America; it was a dream come true. I thought, *Now I am going to get a chance to be educated and to do everything I want!* Everything was so different though. The language was different, and so was the weather. I had seen a few white people before, but never so many, and I had never seen a black person before. Everyone was so tall and confident that it scared me. And they never got hit. When I had walked down the streets in my country, men would hit their wives and their children, but in America, no one did that.

In school I had to speak if I wanted to learn, so for the first time in ten years, I answered questions. Around that time, I also took a health class, and they educated us about sexual abuse. That was the first time I knew what happened to me with those men. I had been *raped*.

At home my stepfather continued to drink and to beat my mother. The only way I could escape it was to get married, because that was an acceptable reason to leave home in my culture. So I looked for a Cambodian guy I could marry, and I found one. He was kind of cute, and when I told him I wanted to get out of my house, he said he would marry me.

I was around fifteen years old when we ran away together. Once we slept together, our families recognized it as a marriage even though we never had a wedding. While we were away at school, my mom continued to get beaten by my stepfather. Sometimes we'd come home and find her bloodied from the beatings she'd taken. My husband and I didn't know what to do. We didn't call the police in our culture. So we kept quiet, and we moved home to help Mom out.

I eventually dropped out of high school and started working for cash under the table. Now that I was earning money, I was able to buy a bigger place for my husband and myself, plus my mom and my sisters. My stepfather would still find us and come back to beat up my mom, me, and even my husband. I never could understand why. I felt powerless to stop it.

Then I got pregnant and my world fell apart.

Lying in the hospital bed after giving birth, the nurse said, "Congratulations, you have a son!"

"No, I don't have a son. I have a daughter."

"No, honey, you have a — "

"I don't want that son. You go get me a daughter. I don't want a son!" All I could think about was what having a son meant. *I have a monster. He is going to grow up and rape someone. He is going to abuse someone. I've got to kill him.* Dark thoughts flooded my mind.

Of course, the nurse couldn't understand and wanted to make things better. "I'll go get him so you can see him."

The nurse brought him in and put him in my arms. But despite my bitterness, I felt love for him and experienced the euphoria of being a first-time mother. But at the same time, I somehow hated him; I couldn't accept that he was male, because I hated men. Then I decided the only answer was for me to kill both of us.

Not long after he was born, I started hearing voices speaking inside my head. I heard my father talking to me. My evil thoughts increased. I experienced flashbacks, remembering faces exploding, dead bodies, and the men who took me to their beds. The thoughts and voices would come and go. I had no idea that it was post-traumatic stress disorder. I thought my only way out was to kill myself, and I hated myself enough to do it.

I thought my only way out was to kill myself, and I hated myself enough to do it.

I went to the pharmacy and bought over-the-counter sleeping pills. I took fifty of them. My family found me and took me to the emergency room. I was put in a psychiatric hospital for a while, and then they released me. The second time I tried to kill myself, I took a hundred pills. It still wasn't enough.

My husband was the greatest guy on earth. He was very kind, and he never hit me. He would never argue, and though I would argue with him, he never even raised his voice. But still, I felt I couldn't go on living.

Every six months or so I would make another attempt to kill myself. I often tried around Mother's Day. I would always get depressed in May. The last time I tried, I took three hundred sleeping pills. When my mother found me, blood was flowing from my eyes, nose, mouth, ears — everywhere. She thought I was dead. They took me to the hospital, and three days later I woke up. I couldn't believe it. I was still alive.

I stayed in the hospital for three months. I wanted to die, but I wasn't allowed to. Why was I so hated? I didn't understand America. What was wrong with this country? In my country, if somebody said they wanted to die, everyone would say, "What are you waiting for? You don't know how? We'll help you." But here they rushed you to the hospital. I thought this was a free country, but what freedom do you have if you can't die when you want to?

Even death didn't seem to want me. I had to try something else. During that time, I learned about the AIDS epidemic on television, so I thought, *If I can get myself infected by disease, I can die that way.*

So I became unfaithful to my husband.

I would sleep with anyone and everyone. When I got pregnant, I would have an abortion. But I still didn't catch a disease.

By the time my son turned four, I had tried to kill myself six times and had nine abortions. After the last attempt, my son, Ricky, asked, "Mommy, why do you hate yourself? Why do you want to die?"

"I don't know," I said. "I don't know."

"Mommy, you beautiful. Love yourself; then you will want to live."

After that, I stopped trying to overdose, but I continued with the infidelity. But I still wasn't a loving mother to Ricky. I was cold, almost devoid of emotion. I didn't know how to give or receive love and affection. One day I said to my husband, "I don't think I love you. Even if I do, I don't know how. I am not good, and I don't know how to change that. We have to go our separate ways."

He didn't want to, but he said, "I love you, and if this is your way, then we will separate."

I couldn't afford to pay rent on my own, so I rented a room to a mother with two grown children from Mexico. Ricky lived with me, but he would come and go between his father and me. About eight months later, I met a married man, and we started seeing each other.

The Mexican family I rented to were Christians, so I decided to try and convert them to Buddhism, the religious tradition I had grown up with. But the mother kept talking to me about Jesus. She knew about the situation with my husband and that I was also dating a married man. Although she was very kind and gentle, she would tell me, "What you are doing is wrong."

I didn't understand her, and I thought she had no right being in my business. From then on, I tried to avoid her, but since we also worked together, it was hard.

One Sunday afternoon, I dragged myself home after being out all night. When I got there, the family was in the kitchen talking and singing.

"Where were you?" the mother asked.

"I was out somewhere. What have you been doing?"

"We went to church, and it was exciting." Then she offered an invitation. "You have to come to church with us. You're not doing anything; why don't you just come? If you don't like it, you never have to go back."

"That's very kind, but no thank you."

I rushed to my room and vowed to try harder to avoid them.

But the same thing happened on Wednesday evening. They were in the kitchen when I walked in. They had been at a church service, and they were still praising God. I cooked my dinner and then finished. "Good-bye," I said as they got up to go to their room. "Um, by the way, I want to go to church with you on Sunday."

Why did I say that? I tried to take it back, but I couldn't. As soon as the mother heard me say it, she started jumping up and down.

"Hallelujah!"

I ran to my room and began pacing. *Why did you do that?*

From where I lived, it took two hours to get to their church in Queens. When we entered the church, they wanted to sit down front, but I insisted on sitting in the back. I shook like a leaf. I didn't want to be there. *If the Buddhists knew you were here right now, you would be in big trouble. You already have enough problems.*

I decided to pray to Buddha. *Buddha, I really love you. I was born a Buddhist, and I'm going to die a Buddhist.* But I decided to talk to Jesus too. *Jesus, I don't know who you are, and I want you to know I'm not here because I am seeking anything. I am just here because I am bored. I don't have anything else to do. I am here to waste time. I am not here to look for you. But I see all these people, and they say that you are God. If you are, you will have to show me.*

> **All these people say that you are God. If you are, you will have to show me.**

After church the family said, "We'll take you to the fellowship."

"Can't we just go home?"

But they insisted. At the fellowship, everyone was very nice, but I must not have looked well, because people came up and said, "We should pray for her; she looks sick." As soon as it was over, I ran out the door.

"Wait!" the daughter called. "My mom is old, and she can't walk fast."

But I had to get out of there.

I was quiet the whole way home. I was angry with them and angry with myself. But they were so happy. I couldn't understand it. Why would people go and listen to music and the pastor and then give their hard-earned money away? I remembered my mom saying that people in church just take your money.

That Wednesday it was the same scene all over again. I came in, and they were all sitting in the kitchen praising God. I heard myself say, "Oh, by the way, I'm coming to church with you this Sunday."

Okay, Terry, I thought, *shut up! You don't want to go to church.*

"Oh, I'm so sorry," the mother said. "We can't go to church this Sunday."

"No problem," I heard myself say. "You just give me directions."

Saturday came, and I said to myself, *I am not going!* Yet I still got up, got dressed, and went to church. This time I felt the need to sit in the front of the church. I sat just as they began singing. Then, for some reason, I pictured that baby on the road in Cambodia as we drove away in the cart. I started to cry. I hadn't cried since the day we had left the baby behind more than twenty years ago. *You don't cry, Terry. You can't cry. That is a weakness!* But I couldn't control it. I just sobbed.

Inside of me, everything hurt. I felt as if my heart was broken into a trillion little pieces. *Why am I so empty? So lonely? So hurt?*

Suddenly it seemed as if Jesus was sitting next to me. I leaned into his shoulder and poured out all my pain as his arms seemed to wrap around me. I cried all through the singing and all through the preaching. I didn't pay attention to anything that was going on around me. I just wanted to keep my head buried in his shoulder.

The pastor said his last prayer, and everyone sang. Then they were done, and everyone started to leave. But my life had changed. I had peace — a peace like I had never known before. I had no more tears, and there was no more pain in my heart. Everything was just gone.

The people around me had no idea what had just happened inside of me. They just smiled and said, "God bless you" or "Have a great day."

When I got home, the family was in their room. I banged on their door and loudly asked, "What happened to me?"

"Calm down," said the mother. "What happened?"

I explained everything.

Then the mother and daughter explained Jesus and his love for me.

That night as I lay in bed, I somehow sensed that I had conceived a child from one of my sexual encounters. Ten days later I would find out that I was right. But that night I heard a voice inside of me say, "Terry, I am here, and I have always loved you." It comforted me.

The next Sunday, I got up and went to church. And the one after that. And the one after that. I would go to church empty and come home full. I had never felt so secure and comforted, because I had never known the love of Jesus. In January I confessed Jesus as my Savior, and a year later I got baptized. My life began to change. Now, instead of wanting to die, I wanted to live.

But for nearly a year, I hid the fact that I was going to church from my family. I didn't want them to know about all the changes that were taking place inside of me. But I couldn't hide my pregnancy. I'd already had nine abortions, and I thought about getting rid of this baby also, but for some reason, I couldn't do it. The woman who lived with me encouraged me to keep it.

"No, you can't have an abortion. That's a baby growing inside of you!"

I decided to keep the baby. Four months later, I gave birth to a beautiful daughter.

As I came to understand more about Jesus and how he works, I began to look over my life and see how God had been there, protecting me even during the worst times of my life, even when I tried to take my life. But I had a lot to heal from because so much damage had been done. Eventually my husband and I divorced and went our separate ways.

I moved in with my mother. Now I was the only Christian living in a house full of Buddhists, and that put a strain on me. Often the only Christian fellowship I had was with God. I started attending the Brooklyn Tabernacle, and eventually my daughter also accepted the Lord.

God took away my broken heart, every pain I ever felt. I am not perfect, but the Lord is changing me as I depend on him every day. I discovered that I am a good cook, and now I work as a private chef for a family in Manhattan. At church I am the head cook for a homeless ministry, and God uses my ability to cook for his glory.

Through the grace of God, I have forgiven those who hurt me when I was young, and now through the power of the Spirit, I want to reach out to young girls in Cambodia and Thailand who are victims of the sex trade. I've been praying and working to raise money. I hope to return one day and give my testimony of Jesus and what he has done to change and heal me. My scars are no longer reminders of a painful life but arrows that daily point me to Jesus. I wouldn't change my past for anything, because if I didn't have my past, I wouldn't love my Lord the way I do now.

Chapter 16

WE OVERCOME FEAR

A film crew and I were at the Brooklyn Heights Promenade, a pedestrian walkway that overlooks the East River in downtown Brooklyn, to tape the companion DVD for this book. But we had time to kill as we waited for it to get dark and for the lights from the southern tip of Manhattan to become visible. While the film crew arranged the lights and got the cameras in position, I noticed that a small group of people had stopped to watch. They probably thought we were shooting a commercial or wondered if I was someone famous. They stood watching and waiting, some licking ice cream cones, while we prepared to film the next segment.

Downtown Brooklyn has become a very trendy spot, and as is often the case with trendy places, it isn't exactly the Bible Belt. Some might even call it godless, due to the hostility of many neighborhoods toward Christian churches and their message. As I waited for my cue, I knew that my next sentences were going to address how life doesn't work unless we know Jesus Christ as Savior and the Holy Spirit empowers us. I was born and raised in Brooklyn, and I strongly sensed that these spectators wouldn't be thrilled with what I was going to say.

Just because I am a pastor doesn't mean I am any different from anyone else. I have the same desire to be liked, to fit in with everyone else. I am not immune to the temptation of fear. At that moment, as I thought about what I would say, and how much the crowd wouldn't want to hear it, a silent but strong pressure came over me. Because I didn't want to be sneered at, cowardice was tempting me. But I fought it. I asked the Lord for help. "God, don't let me hold back in speaking for you because of possible hostility from these people."

The camera lights came on, the director counted down, "Three, two, one," and he gave me the cue. I started talking.

My lines took just two minutes, but the reaction of the crowd took even less time. As soon as I mentioned Jesus, some of the people dropped their heads and walked away. When I mentioned salvation, others brazenly stared at me as if to say, "Are you out of your mind?" By the time I finished talking, not one person from the crowd was left. But I got the words out. I spoke boldly about Jesus Christ as the Savior of the world.

Dealing with Fear

Fear presents itself in many ways — fear of rejection, opposition, suffering, and failure to name a few. But regardless of the ways we encounter fear in our lives, the Holy Spirit can help us overcome it.

FEAR OF REJECTION

Downtown Brooklyn isn't the only place resistant to the gospel. As Christians, we can find hostility wherever we go. That opposition can cause us to become fearful and timid. At times, we all fear rejection. We're afraid that if we stand for Christ, if we speak for Christ, we might not fit in with our family, friends, or coworkers. That's why Scripture warns us about the importance of public confession of our faith in Christ. We can't have it both ways — either we turn our backs on Jesus to escape ridicule, or we embrace our faith no matter the reaction of others. "Whoever is ashamed of me and my words, the Son of Man will be ashamed of them when he comes in his glory and in the glory of the Father and of the holy angels" (Luke 9:26). What a sobering thought that Jesus might be *ashamed* of some of us when he returns to earth.

This need for boldness applies even to kids who grow up in a

Christian home. They go to church, attend Sunday school or Christian camps, and have friends who are believers. They can talk about spiritual things without experiencing much resistance. But things change when they reach high school and later go off to college. Suddenly they find that if they talk about God the Creator, or worse, Jesus dying for the sins of the world, they're labeled. Professors call them ignorant; students brand them as intolerant. Christian students quickly learn that talking about their faith can make them socially unpopular, so some keep quiet, fearing the rejection of their peers.

> **Through the Holy Spirit, God has promised to give us courage, and even boldness, to swim against the current.**

When Christian students leave school and enter the workforce, they find a similar hostility. Now they learn that mentioning Jesus at work may even cause them to lose career opportunities. Again, because of fear, some gradually become closet Christians.

We live in a hostile spiritual environment, and we don't have to be young to face the pressure of giving in to fear or timidity. It's true for ministers as well as for people in the pew. That's why this promise from the Bible is so important for us: "For the Spirit God gave us does not make us timid, but gives us power" (2 Tim. 1:7). Through the Holy Spirit, God has promised to give us courage, and even boldness, to swim against the current and to speak for Christ even though we might be mocked.

FEAR OF OPPOSITION

We have many believers in our congregation who once lived pretty crazy lives. Perhaps they were involved in criminal activities, drugs, or other self-destructive behaviors. What is interesting is that there seems to be a pattern in so many of their stories. While they lived a destructive lifestyle, their family was there to support them. But once they put their faith in Jesus and became born-again Christians, their families often turned against them. When they didn't live for God, when they used drugs, wasted money, got arrested, and who knows what else, their families never bothered them. But once they started following Christ and attending church regularly, their families started to exert emotional pressure on them.

"What? Do you think you're better than us?"

"The church is just after your money."

"What are you in, some kinda cult?"

A great pastor in another part of the city was once a wild, middle-class drug abuser until Christ transformed his life. What a surprise to him when he excitedly told an uncle, "I found Jesus!" and his uncle cynically replied, "Really? I didn't know he was lost."

In the previous chapter, Terry Khem told her dramatic story of becoming a Christian. She had grown up in a Buddhist family, and for the first year of her new faith, she hid it from her family. She was afraid of their rejection. Then when she overcame her fear and told them, she faced a great deal of opposition as the only Christian in a house full of Buddhists. Sometimes she sat in her car to pray just to avoid the battles she faced inside her own home.

But we don't have to be a Buddhist immigrant or a recovering drug addict to face opposition to our faith within our own homes. It happens in stable, otherwise loving homes across this country every day. And that's not even mentioning the opposition that awaits us when we leave our homes. Without courage and boldness from the Holy Spirit, the battle can't be won. The Spirit's invisible but powerful strength will help us live a life worthy of our Lord.

With the Holy Spirit's help, we can experience the same courage that God gave to the early believers. They were threatened by the very authorities who had arranged the crucifixion of Jesus. Upon their release from jail, they gathered with other believers in a prayer meeting (always a good idea when we're faced with an assault on our faith). "After they prayed, the place where they were meeting was shaken. And they were all filled with the Holy Spirit and *spoke the word of God boldly*" (Acts 4:31, emphasis added). Praise God! They felt the heat, but through a time of prayer, they experienced a fresh infilling of the Spirit and a new boldness.

FEAR OF SUFFERING

But let's be honest — other than going through the emotional suffering of rejection or opposition, there isn't a lot of deep suffering for Christ in North America. At least not the kind of suffering faced by the early church. But it is a different story in other parts of the world.

Recently I was invited to be a part of a leadership conference in Hong Kong. Hundreds of church leaders from mainland China attended the conference. It was a unique event in many ways, and participants were there to receive encouragement, instruction in the Word of God, and lessons in apologetic techniques.

The communist regime had for a long time tried to wipe out Christianity; in fact, they have often tried to erase any mention of God. But a church movement has been growing miraculously for many decades in China. Despite the threats and danger, the body of Christ there has grown strong and vibrant. There are now tens of millions of Christians in China.

To lead a Chinese church requires a great deal of courage and boldness. I was told that probably half of the participants had served time in prison, just for serving Christ! As I heard them worship and watched them pray, I felt unworthy to be there.

One morning before I was to speak, they lifted their voices in Mandarin, singing praises to God. I watched as they poured out their hearts in song. Then my interpreter translated some of the words for me. The gist of the chorus went something like this:

> Since you died for us,
> We now offer ourselves to die for you.
> Since you gave yourself on the cross,
> How can we do less than give ourselves for you?
> So, come what may,
> Whether we live or we may die for you,
> We belong to you.

That's not the typical praise and worship song we sing in North America every Sunday, is it? Singing those words and meaning them takes great courage. It was sung by Christian leaders who knew the meaning of suffering for Christ. Some of the most courageous believers today are found in Asia and in Muslim countries where suffering for Jesus is a real possibility. Think of those Pakistani believers I mentioned earlier who are surrounded by daily threats and hatred. How do Christians under such opposition stand so boldly for the Lord Jesus Christ? They stand only through the Holy Spirit, who was given to the church so that bold witness for Christ could be made no matter what the outcome.

FEAR OF FAILURE

Many of us feel prompted to do something for God, but we hold back because we're afraid to fail. A fear of failure stops us from starting the very thing God has laid on our hearts. It might be to join a ministry in our church (or even start one), share a Bible passage with someone on the phone, or perhaps start a prayer meeting. We know it is a prompting from the Lord. But that means leaving our comfort zone and stepping out into uncharted waters.

Consider the building of the temple in Jerusalem. King David wanted to create a magnificent building for God, but the Lord told him that he wouldn't be the one to do it. Instead, the Lord chose his son, Solomon. All of the officials of Israel gathered in Jerusalem, and David announced God's plan. "Of all my sons — and the LORD has given me many — he has chosen my son Solomon to sit on the throne of the kingdom of the LORD over Israel. He said to me: 'Solomon your son is the one who will build my house and my courts'" (1 Chron. 28:5 – 6).

God's choice was clear. Seems simple, right? David had already received the building plans from God himself and collected most of the needed materials. All Solomon had to do was *start*. But right there is so often the place of failure. David understood the challenge facing his son. Throughout the chapter we find him encouraging Solomon: "Be strong and do the work" (v. 10). And "Be strong and courageous, and do the work. Do not be afraid or discouraged, for the LORD God, my God, is with you. He will not fail you or forsake you until all the work for the service of the temple of the LORD is finished" (v. 20).

Many of us feel prompted to do something for God, but we hold back because we're afraid to fail. Despite the facts that Solomon was God's choice and that he had complete instructions and all of the needed materials, he still had to get past the fear that paralyzes us to inaction. *The Message*, a contemporary Bible translation, renders verse 10, "And do it!" No one is saying that there won't be opposition or problems, but it is through the Spirit's impartation of faith and boldness that we can be brave and move ahead with the work God has called us to do.

God has called all of us to something. Remember what Jesus said about the moment he will return? "Be on guard! Be alert! You do not know when that time will come. It's like a man going away: He leaves his house and puts his servants in charge, *each with their assigned task*, and tells the one at the door to keep watch" (Mark 13:33 – 34, emphasis added). But because of fear, we haven't always gone out and *done* it. Just because there is an "assigned task" doesn't mean it will automatically get accomplished. Nor does it mean it will be easy.

Whether building a temple, leading an underground church in the face of government opposition, or simply speaking the truth in front of a crowd in Brooklyn, we have all faced challenges from fear. But the Holy Spirit is greater in power than our shyness or timidity. And he is greater than our fear of rejection or failure. His power makes the weakest as bold as a lion (Prov. 28:1).

Be Bold in the Spirit

Paul wrote to a young pastor named Timothy about the promise of a bold, fearless Christianity through the indwelling Spirit. Timothy came from a family of believers. Both his grandmother and his mother were Christians before him (2 Tim. 1:5), so Timothy came from a faith-filled background. He was the spiritual son of the apostle Paul and eventually entered the ministry. Obviously Timothy enjoyed great spiritual privileges from the very day of his conversion.

But despite all those early advantages and godly examples, something was amiss with Timothy's ministry. Thus Paul challenged him, "I remind you to fan into flame the gift of God, which is in you through the laying on of my hands. For the Spirit God gave us does not make us timid, but gives us power" (2 Tim. 1:6 – 7).

Paul reminds Timothy, and all of us, that we can be sincere in our faith and yet drift back away from a bold spiritual position into fear and timidity. Even Christians who love the Lord and study the Bible can be fearful and self-conscious when opportunities to speak for Christ arise. Sadly, in some situations, we seemingly can speak about anything but our Savior.

So what did Paul tell him to do? Did he tell him to try harder, to reach down for something deeper within?

No.

Paul told Timothy that the Holy Spirit was the only antidote to the virus of fear in his life. The Spirit's fire had to be stirred up — nurtured and given attention to — for when God's Spirit was ablaze, there would be boldness to replace Timothy's seemingly natural inclination to timidity. And now, two thousand years later, church history has clearly shown that when God's Spirit moves, when believers and churches meet God in a new way, people become bold and radical for Jesus Christ. It is not something taught by a Christian minister. Spiritual courage only comes directly from the Holy Spirit.

Take Courage!

Spiritual courage is the great need for so many of us today. We may have heard great teaching and read multiple translations of the Bible. But what we need to do is to "stir up" the work of the Spirit within us. We must give ourselves afresh to God in prayer, Bible reading, and a new yielding to the Holy Spirit. We must also separate ourselves from thoughts, words, and actions that hinder the Spirit's flow. In the words of Scripture, "Come near to God and he will come near to you" (James 4:8).

If we humbly draw near for a new intimacy with God, will he turn us away? Will he deny us the blessings we ask for? If he gave us Jesus while we were yet sinners, will he now as our heavenly Father reject our petitions for more of the Spirit's boldness and courage? That would deny everything we know about him from Scripture!

How many believers come to the end of their lives and feel as if they somehow missed the fullness of God's plan for their lives? They think that perhaps God had something more planned, but it eluded them. This is a sad thought. But if we allow the Spirit to move through us, we will see his plans and purposes accomplished. We won't come to the end of our lives regretting so many missed opportunities to do more for Christ.

Our future will be determined by how we allow God the Holy Spirit to work in and through us. We can live our days out in fearful hesitation and second-guessing, or we can "let go and let God." God's plan for us is not about who we are and what talents we bring to the table. It's about the resources and grace God has promised us.

So we say with confidence,

"The Lord is my helper: I *will not be afraid.*
    What can mere mortals do to me?"
        Hebrews 13:6, emphasis added

Chapter 17

WE CAN SHAKE THE KINGDOM WITH OUR PRAYERS

It was just before dawn on a chilly day in Palestine about two thousand years ago. Jesus' disciples were sound asleep, exhausted after the previous day's activities — handling the huge crowds that had thronged them, encouraging listeners to believe the Master's words, even trying their hand at praying for a few of the sick and brokenhearted. But while they enjoyed their needed rest, someone else was stirring. Although the sun had not yet risen, Jesus got up and walked out of the village where they were all staying. He was headed to a deserted place nearby to pray.

What an awesome scene! It was repeated many times during the three years the disciples stayed with Jesus. The Son of the living God couldn't face the day without prayer.

Jesus habitually offered up prayers, sometimes with "fervent cries and tears" (Heb. 5:7). His prayers enabled him to make decisions and face the challenges and demonic attacks that confronted him daily. This isn't a new believer in Christ we're talking about; it is Jesus Christ the Holy One himself! If he felt the need to talk with his Father, how much more necessary it must be for us — if we only realize it.

As Samuel Chadwick, a great Methodist preacher of late-nineteenth-to-early-twentieth-century England, wrote: "God and prayer are inseparable.... The teaching of the Old Testament is full of the subject of prayer. Everywhere there are commands and inducements to pray, and the great stories of deliverance and victory, experience and vision, are all examples of prevailing prayer.... There are many problems about prayer, but they lie outside the fact and experience of prayer, and *apart from praying* there is no solution to them."[1]

To the person who truly prays, there is no problem reconciling God's sovereignty with a heartfelt petition. Again, remember that Scripture declares: "You do not have because you do not ask God" (James 4:2). It wasn't that God didn't desire to give an answer or that some divine decree stood against us. If we missed out, it was because we didn't have the faith, time, and spiritual temperament to talk with our Father.

Our Pestering Prayers Can Save Others

Remember the story of Abraham and his nephew Lot? They had separated in Canaan because their large herds couldn't all be fed and nourished in the same area. Abraham let the younger man choose first the land he wanted. Lot quickly decided to move east toward the rich plains near Sodom and Gomorrah. Lot should have prayed for God's will in the matter, but his eyes betrayed him. He would soon discover that good appearances can be deceiving.

Sometime later Abraham encountered the Angel of the Lord and learned that news of Sodom's gross wickedness had reached heaven. Judgment seemed inevitable, and Abraham's heart turned quickly to the predicament of his nephew Lot. Then, in one of the most incredible portions of the Bible (Gen. 18:16 – 33), Abraham, this great man of faith, commenced to negotiate with the Lord (the Angel of the Lord is identified with deity in Old Testament Scripture) that Sodom be spared from destruction. Of course, Lot was really on his mind, but Abraham never mentioned his name. "Will you sweep away the righteous with the wicked?" Abraham asked. "What if there are fifty righteous people in the city?" (vv. 23 – 24). The Lord heard Abraham's plea, for he agreed to spare the city if fifty godly people existed.

But Abraham wasn't done. "How about if there are forty-five?" Then he pleaded for Sodom to be spared if forty righteous people could be found. Why didn't the Lord just tell him that he had already predestined the future of Sodom and Lot with it? Instead, the Angel of the Lord went along with the man's persistent pleading. Finally, Abraham whittled the number to ten righteous people. This kind of pestering prayer seems a bit over the line, don't you think? But the Lord seemed pleased rather than being put off with Abraham's argument.

It was too late for Sodom though. Two angels were sent there and discovered just how ugly and out of hand things had gotten (Gen. 19:1 – 13). The angels emphatically warned Lot and his family to get out of town immediately. There was no time to waste; judgment was imminent. But then Lot began to waver and hesitate. It was difficult for him to leave all the good stuff he'd accumulated. The angelic beings were forced to grasp the hands of Lot, his wife, and two daughters, and firmly guide them away from ground zero. Lot's family would find safety in the nearby town of Zoar, but they must "flee there quickly" because the angels "cannot do anything until you reach it" (Gen. 19:22).

The end of the story is sad, but here's the silver lining: "Early the next morning Abraham got up and returned to the place where he had stood before the LORD. He looked down toward Sodom and Gomorrah, toward all the land of the plain, and he saw dense smoke rising from the land, like smoke from a furnace. So when God destroyed the cities of the plain, *he remembered Abraham*, and *he brought Lot out of the catastrophe* that overthrew the cities where Lot had lived" (Gen. 19:27 – 29, emphasis added).

Why did the angels forcibly remove Lot's family from doomed Sodom? Why couldn't the command for destruction be given until Lot reached safety? It sure wasn't because Lot and his family were spiritually sensitive and prayerful; the man almost fought off two angels trying to rescue him! No, the lesson of the whole strange story is this: God remembered and honored Abraham's prayers for his nephew, and because of them, he saved Lot from a catastrophe. Lot's family was spared for one reason alone: an old man prayed for him and prevailed with God Almighty.

Prayer Links Us to Power

This story seems very foreign to what most of us think about prayer. We have unfortunately formed our ideas not from Scripture, illuminated by the Holy Spirit, but rather from what we have seen and experienced in our churches. And that is often not a very faith-inspiring model for us to follow. Just as we neglect the person of the Holy Spirit, we also neglect or gloss over the idea that prayer can secure answers from God. "It is a concept from another day, another time," we say. Yet when we consider Jesus' prayer life and the amazing deliverance granted through Abraham's intercession, we easily understand why Satan targets corporate and individual prayer. He doesn't like when we gather to sing praises, study God's Word, and fellowship together. But if we ever commit to giving ourselves over to *real prayer*, the kind that moves mountains, well, then all the enemy's heavy guns will be brought out against us. After all, prayer links us to the promises and power of the Almighty.

Prayer links us to the promises and power of the Almighty.

This powerful weapon in our spiritual warfare is first mentioned in Genesis when "people began to call on the name of the Lord" (Gen. 4:26). Thousands of years later, the apostle Paul declared that the Lord "richly blesses all who call on him, for, 'Everyone who calls on the name of the Lord will be saved'" (Rom. 10:12 – 13). Calling out to God threatens Satan's kingdom because it brings the blessings of heaven to earth and grants salvation to the ungodly.

Oswald Chambers said: "The prayer of the feeblest saint who lives in the Spirit and keeps right with God is a terror to Satan. The very powers of darkness are paralyzed by prayer; no spiritualistic séance can succeed in the presence of a humble praying saint. No wonder Satan tries to keep our minds fussy in active work till we cannot think in prayer."

It's easy to understand how prayers can be stopped in public schools filled with unbelieving students and teachers. But when God's own people and Christian churches have little or no time for prayer, that's another story. The angels must weep when they see our disinterest in prayer! Do we realize we're forfeiting the help and strength promised by a faithful God to those who will simply take time to ask?

The early church devoted itself to prayer (Acts 2:42) and even prayed Peter out of prison the night before his scheduled execution (Acts 12). The first time the believers were persecuted, they met together in corporate prayer and "raised their voices together" (Acts 4:24). God responded by granting them a fresh filling of the Holy Spirit and a boldness to witness for Christ.

After Saul was blinded by his Damascus Road encounter with Jesus, he was visited by Ananias. Through a vision, the Lord had informed Ananias that Saul, the church's archenemy, had converted to the Way. But Ananias was still fearful, so God gave him definitive proof of Saul's salvation, saying, "Behold, he is praying" (Acts 9:11 NKJV). It sometimes seems that God divides humankind into two simple categories, folks who pray to him and those who don't.

Lifting Our Hearts to a God Who Can Be Trusted

I think most of us are aware that Jesus insisted that his followers "always pray and not give up" (Luke 18:1). And although his disciples never once asked him for lessons in preaching, they did ask, "Lord, teach us to pray" (Luke 11:1). They were aware of what we might call "the spiritual secret" behind Jesus' life and ministry. When they requested his help to pray, I think they were asking not only what prayer looked like — what to say — but also how they could be inspired to do it and persevere in it. They wanted to practice daily prayer just like their Master. It's all too easy to admire from afar the power of prayer and understand the promises attached to it without ever experiencing its reality in our lives.

At its core, prayer is not about the words that are spoken. Rather, it's about uplifting our hearts to a God who can be trusted. It's not about religious-sounding phrases, since tears and groans often receive the strongest responses. It is primitive and heart-centered, which is what makes it so unacceptable to many refined, intellectually proud believers and churches. In its purest form, prayer has a raw fervency and faith that prevails with God and secures answers otherwise thought impossible.

As we have learned, "Love one another" and "Rejoice always" can only be obeyed through the power of the Holy Spirit. As Andrew Bonar, a nineteenth-century minister from Scotland, once masterfully said, "All merit is in the Son; all power is by the Spirit." Our acceptance and salvation are always through the grace of Christ and his cross, but at the same time, all obedience to God is only possible through the Spirit's enablement. And that is also true for the kind of praying we see in Scripture — the Holy Spirit makes it possible. To see that, we only need to compare our hollow habits of merely "saying prayers" to Elijah's bold petitions, Moses' intercession for the Israelites, or Paul's travail like a mother giving birth.

When witnessing to a nonbeliever, many of us rely on the power of the Spirit to open the mind and heart of the listener, so why don't we rely on that same Spirit when we pray? "Why do you suppose it is that so little stress is laid on the influences of the Spirit in prayer when so much is said about His influences in conversion?" asked Charles Finney. "Many people are amazingly afraid the Spirit's influences will be left out. They lay great stress on the Spirit's influences in converting sinners. But how little is said, how little is printed, about His influence in prayer! How little complaining there is that people do not make enough of the Spirit's influence in leading Christians to pray according to the will of God! Let it never be forgotten that no Christian ever prays aright, unless led by the Spirit."[2]

Spirit-Enabled Prayer

The apostle Paul, writer of most of the New Testament, made an extraordinary admission in Romans: "In the same way, the Spirit helps us in our weakness. We do not know what we ought to pray for, but the Spirit himself intercedes for us through wordless groans" (8:26). Notice the key phrases:

- "We do not know what we ought to prayer for." That is written in first person plural — Paul included himself! The mightiest apostle in history didn't know how to properly pray?
- "The Spirit helps us in our weakness." Are we really all so spiritually frail that we need assistance from God to simply pray the right way?
- "The Spirit helps us." All power is in the Holy Spirit, including the grace to pray right so God can hear and answer.

The Spirit helps us *to do prayer*, to get away from the bustle of life and get alone with God. He reveals our critical need of daily grace by contrasting God's strength with our human frailty. He tenderly reminds us of our structural vulnerability to temptation, our cowardice, and our unkind reactions to people and situations. He draws us gently to our Source and helps our hearts to sincerely bow, believe, and petition at God's throne. The Spirit readjusts our priorities based on eternal values; and by helping us to be spiritually minded, he convinces us of our overwhelming need to talk with our Father.

The Spirit readjusts our priorities based on eternal values.

We all know there are things we should never pray about because they dishonor God or don't comply with his holy instructions. It would be utter foolishness to pray, "God, should I cheat on my income tax form or not? Guide me in the path I should follow." But what about complex questions that don't have answers in Scripture? Many times we face situations in life that are quite complicated and we are unsure what we should pray for — there is no obvious right or wrong choice. Maybe an opportunity arises for a short-term mission trip, a rebellious child gets in trouble with the law, or a pastoral staff faces the possibility of a move to a larger facility and it will involve raising millions of dollars. What is God's will in those situations? How should we pray? That is where the Holy Spirit helps us by revealing God's will and granting us the faith to pray in the right direction.

The prayer of faith moves mountains (Mark 11:23 – 24; James 5:15). The Spirit alone makes the power of God so real to our inner person that we are enabled to ask, seek, and knock with bold assurance. This is another reason why the deepest truths and secrets of prayer can never be learned by lectures, teaching tapes, or books (including this one!). Prayer is learned by praying, and the heart usually learns faster than the head. "So then faith *comes* by hearing, and hearing by the word of God" (Rom. 10:17 NKJV). The Holy Spirit marries prayer and faith together within us, and the results are life changing.

Let the Spirit Blow

The Holy Spirit *is* the spirit of true prayer; he is both its origin and its lifeblood. That's why we must be careful, individually and corporately, not to grieve him.

I spoke some time ago at a large leadership conference where sincere men and women gathered to have their spiritual batteries recharged. I felt God's anointing as I delivered his Word, and then I concluded by calling forward all those who desired fresh grace to help them fulfill their callings. Hundreds responded, and soon there was an awe-filled sense of the Spirit's presence. Fervent, sincere, and humble petitions mingled with tears and audible cries rose heavenward. It was the kind of praying that brought spiritual renewal to churches across the centuries, the kind that replaced lukewarmness with a burning desire to be like Christ and sacrifice everything for him. The Holy Spirit had come to help us pray! No one glanced at his or her watch to see what time it was, because in God's presence, in a sense, time stands still.

Eventually I had to leave the platform to talk with a fellow minister who had been very ill. As I left, people were sitting, kneeling, standing, or lying prostrate on the floor — physical posture is irrelevant when the heart meets God in prayer. But in the midst of all that fervent prayer, someone suddenly took the microphone and ordered everyone back to their seats. "Before the service ends, the choir and orchestra will close with two anthems that will just blow you away!" It was an intrusion of the human element into the gentle work of the Spirit. It must have felt like a punch in the stomach to those who were lost in the sweet presence of Jesus. Anthems, hymns, and sermons all have their place, but not when the Spirit is helping God's children to plead for fresh power. There *is* a time for everything under the sun, but wisdom must help us know what the moment calls for.

I've noticed that church services and conference gatherings are increasingly (and proudly) governed by "tight timelines" as we try to imitate corporate America. A song here, announcements there, move on to this, and keep with the timeline, please. Above all, let's avoid downtime with no one at the mike. Heaven forbid that we'd ever dare to entrust the service or conference to the wind of the Spirit and not know what we're going to do next! The Bible cautions us not to grieve the Holy Spirit — offend, distress, vex, or sadden him. At that leadership conference I spoke at, it sure seemed to many of us that the Holy Spirit was saddened that a conference schedule with choir anthems was a higher priority than following his sovereign, sweet, and much needed ministry.

Praying in the Spirit

Paul told the Ephesians to "pray in the Spirit on all occasions with all kinds of prayers and requests" (Eph 6:18). What an interesting phrase and word picture — *pray in* the Spirit. Pray in, through, and by the Holy Spirit, who is God himself! That's a vital truth and probably one of the least taught subjects in the New Testament. In addition to that reference in Ephesians, there are more references: "So what shall I do? I will pray with my spirit, but I will also pray with my understanding;

I will sing with my spirit, but I will also sing with my understanding" (1 Cor. 14:15). Notice that Paul prays not only with his mind but also with his spirit, stirred and prompted by the Spirit of God.

Where else would the Spirit primarily work but in our human spirits? Also to combat those who divide the body of Christ, those who follow "mere natural instincts and do not have the Spirit," Jude told his leaders to "build yourselves up in your most holy faith and *pray in the Holy Spirit*" (Jude 20, emphasis added).[3]

All those directives about prayer inspired by the Holy Spirit might seem like some kind of emotional fanaticism to some. They feel it's for those "other folks" who always sing too loud and lift their hands in church every six seconds. They say, "That's not how I was raised in church." Does it matter one iota how we were raised and what we saw in our particular denominational cultures? Didn't God give us the Bible so we could prayerfully and humbly search its depths and experience what it promises? Did the Holy Spirit's power to inspire prayer somehow evaporate during the centuries following the book of Acts? Will the Spirit help us today any less, especially when we need him most? This doesn't sound like what a merciful God would do.

Often when I speak at a pastor's conference, a Q&A session follows my presentation. The most common question by far is along the lines of "How can my church become more of a house of prayer?"

In answering, I try to help my listeners understand that being a true "house of prayer" is directly related to the degree to which the Holy Spirit is honored. How will we boldly pray in faith if the Holy Spirit is not helping us? Is it not amazing that some of the best Bible teaching churches are at the same time basically prayerless? Without an understanding of and hunger for the Spirit, prayer will never grow as a dynamic force to secure God's blessings.

> Only as the Spirit leads and inspires will we rise to a new level of prevailing prayer.

The same is true for you and me as individuals. Only as the Spirit leads and inspires will we rise to a new level of prevailing prayer. Then strongholds *will* come down, loved ones *will* be visited by God's grace, and people around us *will* be reminded that Christ is a living Savior and not a mere theological concept. Samuel Chadwick wrote long ago: "We are never really men [and women] of prayer in the best sense until we are 'filled with the Holy Ghost.'"[4]

Recently I met a preteen girl in our BT Kids program. Although she is pretty and intelligent, she barely looked at me when I was introduced to her.

"What's wrong?" I asked.

She didn't pause for a second with her answer. "I'm mad at my mother, my father, my school, God, Jesus — I'm angry with everyone!" I learned gang members were trying to recruit this precious girl who was already fighting against so much. She lived in a tough neighborhood that swallowed kids like her. In addition, she had a difficult and challenging life at home. No one talked to her or tried to understand what she was feeling. I shared with her Jesus' love and plan for her life as best I could, but it seemed as if I got nowhere.

Although I talked and prayed with dozens of people that Sunday, I couldn't get that young lady out of my mind and my heart. Even without pursuing it, I found myself praying daily for her with a deep concern, as if she were my own grandchild.

With so many prayer requests in a church like ours, how do you think that preteen became a main topic of my petitions and intercession? Could Satan, my carnal nature, or the spirit of this selfish world be behind it all? Not hardly. For some reason, the Holy Spirit arranged for me to meet her, and then he deposited a burden of prayer in me so I could fight for a girl whom Christ loves and died for. I didn't ask for that. I wasn't looking for another personal prayer project. But although her battle is far from over, I'm already beginning to see answers to my petitions.

How about you? Do you have a concern for a loved one living too close to Sodom? Abraham stood in between God and his nephew Lot, whom he loved. What a marvelous deliverance Abraham's prayers brought about! Do you have a relative or friend facing eternity without a Savior? Maybe you know a parent or child who seems to get harder by the day and you're wondering what to do. Let's try following God's directive — *prayer*!

God is reminding us that *nothing* is too hard for him. All that's needed are believers yielded to the Spirit's influence so that prayer that shakes the kingdom of darkness can be offered to the glory of Christ.

Lord, teach us to pray, and let it be prayer in the Holy Spirit.

Chapter 18

AN ANSWER TO PRAYER: THE STORY OF ANNES

Awhile ago, our church started a new ministry to special needs children and their parents. Annes Mogoli has been the passion behind that ministry, providing the energy, time, and excitement to get it off the ground and keep it running. She has done a remarkable job with few resources in a ministry that presents new physical and emotional challenges on a weekly basis. But Annes leaves each Sunday wondering what else she can do to serve those children and their families. That is remarkable considering that Annes has a full-time job and she's a single mother raising six kids.

Annes's tireless passion flows from an outpouring of her thankfulness to God for answering her prayers, along with those of our church, when she and her children needed it most.

ANNES

I was twenty-four years old, single, and pregnant, and I didn't want to raise my child under the same negative influences I had growing up. That meant I had to leave Grenada. My parents were both heavy drinkers. My father even forced me to buy alcohol for him while I was still in school. He often said cruel things to me, and I didn't stop him. I was the quiet one in the family, and I didn't speak up for myself.

But for my baby, I wanted more than the kind of life I grew up with. I decided to move to America, hoping that it would give my baby and me a fresh start.

Someone bought me a plane ticket to New York, and my cousin and another friend helped me find a job and get settled. A few months later, I gave birth to a son, and I named him Alex. I found an apartment, and I got a job as a nursing assistant. I was determined to do whatever it took to make my new life work for my son and me.

In the apartment below me lived Roses, a Christian woman who was a nurse. We would talk about work, but she also started telling me about the Lord. She and her daughter would ask me if I wanted to go to church with them. At first I refused. But as my son got older, I decided it would be good for him to go to Sunday school. We went to a little church on Linden Boulevard in Queens. On my first day there, I reached out to Jesus. I wish I could tell you that I walked with the Lord from that day on, but I didn't. I would attend church for a while, then I'd fall away, then go back, and then I'd stop again.

Around that time, I met a handsome man from Nigeria, and we started dating. Eventually he moved in with me. Two pregnancies quickly followed. I gave birth to a son we named Melvin, and then to a daughter we named Ngozi. My friend Roses visited me soon after Ngozi was born. "You're not getting away from me," she said. "I don't care how cold it is outside. Get that baby wrapped up on Sunday, because I'm picking you up and taking you to church."

Though it was unusually cold for a November Sunday, it was warm inside the church — warm from the love of the people. I started attending regularly.

As I learned more about the Bible, I realized that I was in a sinful relationship with my boyfriend. On top of that, he was verbally abusive. He often said things like, "You're so ugly. And you're fat." His hurtful words brought back memories of my father, and his constant verbal abuse robbed me of my self-esteem. But church was different — people hugged me and loved me. And as I grew, I knew it was time to make a change. I prayed to God to help me get out of the life I was living.

But before I could make a change, I was pregnant again and gave birth to my fourth child, a daughter I named Ije. I knew I couldn't leave my boyfriend now. Besides, who would want me? Roses saw how discouraged I was, and she suggested that we start attending prayer meetings at the Brooklyn Tabernacle. I worked near the church, so on Tuesdays I would pay the babysitter extra to keep the kids while I attended the prayer meeting. At those meetings, I opened up my heart to the Lord and cried out to him about my life. On Sundays I attended the regular services, bringing my kids with me to attend the BT Kids services. Once again I knew the way I was living wasn't pleasing the Lord and that I needed to do something about it. I thought perhaps getting a commitment from my boyfriend would fix things.

"I can't live this way anymore," I told him. "It's not right for me to live with a man if I am not married to him."

"Okay, so we'll get married," he said.

I was excited that finally I would get things right before God. And I truly thought that once we were married, things would get better between us, but nothing changed. Even though he was now my husband, he continued to belittle and berate me.

One day he came home and said he'd found a job in New Jersey. He wanted to live there during the week so he could be closer to his office. On weekends he would come home. I was worried. That wasn't the way most marriages worked, and with four kids and a full-time job, I depended on his help on the rare occasions he offered it. But his mind was made up, and I could only agree with his decision. So I worked and took care of the kids by myself during the week.

At least I was still close to my church. It was my faith that sustained me during those exhausting days. God gave me an inner strength, and he guided me on how to be a good mother even though I never had a role model to learn from. For example, his Spirit led me to read to my babies and to tell them about Jesus.

> It was my faith that sustained me during those exhausting days. God gave me an inner strength.

And every time the door was open at church, we were there. God used the people of the Brooklyn Tabernacle to bless me spiritually and occasionally financially.

I got pregnant again, and this time something went terribly wrong during the delivery. I called my husband's home and his office in New Jersey, but I couldn't find him anywhere, so I went to the hospital alone. I could feel something was wrong, yet the doctors went ahead and induced labor. The baby was huge, and when he dropped, he dropped so low that they could no longer do a C-section. And now he was stuck — he was too big to pass through the birth canal on his own. I lay on the table, prayed, and cried out to Jesus.

About that time, the song being played in the delivery room

changed and a new song came on. It was *We Come Rejoicing*, and it was sung by the Brooklyn Tabernacle choir! It was a sign. *Lord, I know you're here with me.* I kept praying silently. Finally, I heard the doctor say, "We have an emergency. We can't get this baby out."

"Jesus!" was all I could say as the pain grew stronger.

Out of the corner of my eye, I saw a figure in the hall. He entered the room and asked for some gloves. I shook from the pain, but somehow the doctor reached in and positioned the baby so that he came out. Elijah was eleven pounds and one ounce. But something had gone wrong during the delivery. As soon as he was out, he began having seizures. Someone asked if I had been using drugs. "No! I've never done drugs," I told them. But they didn't listen, and they took Elijah away from me.

I had four kids at home with a babysitter, my husband couldn't be found, and now they had implied that I was a drug user! I did the only thing I knew to do: I prayed. *Father, you know my heart, and you're my Deliverer. I need you right now. God, I'm going to dedicate this baby to you. When they put him in my arms, I'm going to consecrate him to you right here in the hospital.*

They had taken Elijah away to do drug testing, but before long, they were back. The tests had all been negative. "You can see your baby now," a nurse said.

When I saw Elijah for the first time, he looked like a football player. He was huge! I touched his head and prayed over him. I dedicated his head, his hands, his feet — everything about him — to the Lord.

At the time, they weren't sure what caused the seizures. Later I would find out that his unusual birth had caused trauma. His shoulder had been injured during the delivery, and he sustained damage to his entire left side. Months later, a doctor would diagnose him with Erb's palsy.

Someone at the hospital advised me to call an attorney before I left the hospital. "There's a lot going on here," they warned. I had no idea who to call, but the Holy Spirit prompted me to call the church. They recommended I talk to a woman who sang in the choir. Her name was Esther, and she was an attorney.

Esther filed a lawsuit against the hospital, and it took a long time before they finally settled. But in the meantime, I kept praying for my son. For the first five years of his life, he never spoke a word; he only made noises and drooled. His hands turned under, and he couldn't stretch out his fingers. I prayed and had other people praying for Elijah. And God answered our prayers. The Holy Spirit used other people to direct me to Mount Sinai Medical Center, one of the best hospitals in the world. After lots of therapy, a surgery, and much prayer, the damage was reversed. Today Elijah is a healthy twelve-year-old who won't stop talking! He is in the seventh grade and getting fantastic grades and thriving in every way. Looking back, I now see how God used that time with Elijah to prepare me for what was to come next.

Once again, I got pregnant. The enemy messed with my mind, saying things like, "You can never have this baby. Look at all the problems you have already. Think about how your husband is treating you. How can you have another child?"

At church one morning, I walked into the service with my head hanging down. *I can't let anyone know I am pregnant again.* But during the message, out of nowhere, Pastor Cymbala said, "There's a woman here whom the enemy is attacking in her mind about her pregnancy. But the Lord wants you to know that if you have that baby, you will be blessed." That was the sign I needed. I held my head up high as I left church. Instead of feeling sorry for myself, I spent even more time in prayer, often closing my bathroom door as I wept and called out to the Lord.

A little over a year after Elijah was born, I gave birth to my sixth child, Joel. God continued to use the church to bless me. One night I wanted to come to the prayer meeting in the worst way, but I didn't have any money to get home. I decided to walk, putting Joel in the stroller and having Elijah stand on the back of the stroller. That would get me there, but how would I get home? It would be too dangerous to walk that far at night. All the way there I prayed, "Lord, I want to go to church. You provide a way for me to get back home."

> I cried for joy, because God had answered my prayer.

That night, the pastor said, "I know there are people in desperate financial need here tonight. If you're in need, stand up so the church can pray for you." I stood and lifted my hands. A lady on the other side of the room came over to me and handed me twenty dollars.

"The Lord told me to come and give this to you," she said.

I cried for joy, because God had answered my prayer. I had never met the woman before, and I didn't even learn her name that night. But I did notice that she had a long braid that hung down her back.

Time passed, and we were making it by the grace of God. Joel was almost two and Ngozi, my oldest daughter, was nine when one January morning Ngozi called to me from her bedroom.

"Mommy, Mommy, come quick. I can't walk!"

I rushed in and tried to help her up from the floor. But she really couldn't walk. She had been fine the night before, but that morning she was completely paralyzed. What had happened? What was I supposed to do now? I had already felt overwhelmed. The doctors were still trying to help Elijah, Joel had been diagnosed with asthma and had almost died once, and my husband was of absolutely no help. Now Ngozi couldn't walk? I picked up the phone and called the church. I always called the church before I called the doctor.

I also called Esther, who by now was like a part of the family. She was also an incredible prayer warrior. She called Pastor Cymbala, and together they tried to find a doctor to help Ngozi. Was it a physical injury? Or perhaps some kind of an emotional problem? There had been a lot of stress in our home lately.

I made an appointment with a rheumatologist at Mount Sinai, the center that helped Elijah so much, and they ran a full battery of tests. He even gave her a full body scan, but they couldn't find any cause for her paralysis. They were stumped.

Ngozi started missing a lot of school. Eventually the board of education began questioning me. Then child welfare services started asking questions. No one could believe what was happening to Ngozi, because she had been perfectly healthy and then suddenly couldn't walk. As her condition worsened, the school had to provide a bus for handicapped children to take her to and from school. During the day, they assigned a paraprofessional to move her from room to room and to the bathroom when necessary.

The stress of Ngozi's illness began to take a toll on my marriage. My husband would say some strange things like, "Why did we have all these kids anyway?" I couldn't understand what was going through his mind. During this time, he came home less and less. Eventually he moved to New Jersey permanently, and he divorced me.

I prayed, *Lord, I desperately need you. I'm on my own now. You have to help me to be a good mother, and you have to be my children's Father. And you are going to have to heal Ngozi. You have to heal her.* I don't know how I became so bold in my prayer, other than the fact that I was desperate. *Lord, I am holding on to you, I know you can do this.* I begged God to help see us through all that we were facing.

We continued to come to church, even though it was more difficult with Ngozi's inability to walk. During the week, I would scrimp and save money, and then on Sunday mornings, I would dress all of the kids and take the money I had saved and call a cab. The cab would drop us off, and a man from the church, Big Willy, would meet us at the door, scoop Ngozi in his arms, and carry her to the children's area. When it was time to go home, Willy would call a cab and then get Ngozi from the children's area, bring her down, and gently place her inside the cab. The Holy Spirit always sent me the exact people I needed.

But over time, I got tired. I got very tired. I worked full-time as a nurse's assistant and took Ngozi to therapy appointments at Mount Sinai twice a week. It was important that we continued therapy on her legs so they didn't atrophy. Muscles that aren't used can cause the foot to turn inward, and that was starting to happen. The therapy didn't seem to help much though, and the doctors still didn't know what caused her paralysis. The social workers still suspected some kind of hidden trauma. Caring for her was emotionally and physically exhausting.

One Friday morning in July, Esther called and said, "She's going to walk again. She's going to be healed."

"I'm so tired, Esther," I said, trying to hold back the tears. It had been six months since Ngozi's paralysis, and I could feel my faith slipping. I had spent endless hours in my bathroom, weeping and praying for Ngozi to be healed.

Esther sensed the strain I was under and said, "I can't leave you alone today. I can hear how tired you are." The Holy Spirit prompted her to call her clients and cancel all her appointments. "I'll drive you to the hospital today."

A few hours later, Esther picked us up and drove to the medical center. I could tell she fervently prayed for Ngozi as she drove. When we pulled into the parking lot, Esther said, "I feel the Lord wants me to park the car and walk Ngozi around the block."

I just stared at her. I was too tired to argue. Esther got out of the car and opened the back door. She took Ngozi's hands, and amazingly I saw her leg move a little bit.

"Esther! Her leg is moving!"

Esther praised God. Then, holding Ngozi by the hand, she slowly walked Ngozi around the block tiny step after tiny step. Then we took her upstairs to see the rheumatologist. We told him what happened, but he had no explanation.

After the doctor's appointment, we got back in Esther's car and drove to the church. I wanted to meet with the Prayer Band, a dedicated group of men and women who meet at the church and pray daily for the needs of people in it.

"Annes," Esther said, "God is going to heal her."

"I know," I said. And I believed it.

At the church, we took Ngozi downstairs to where the Prayer Band had gathered. Pastor Ware was there. He laid hands on her and said, "You're going to walk in the name of Jesus!" Then he looked at me and said, "I don't know what this is, but she is released. The chains are broken. Whatever Satan is trying to do is broken today."

"The chains are broken. Whatever Satan is trying to do is broken today."

Prayer Band members placed their hands on Ngozi's legs and cried out for God to heal her body. It was such fervent prayer that I became very emotional. I watched Ngozi's face, and for the first time, I saw hope in her eyes. Although she wasn't healed then, my faith increased through their prayers. She would walk again; I just didn't know when.

On Tuesday I brought Ngozi to the children's prayer meeting. While we were there, the leader explained to the children that Ngozi wasn't able to walk. "Do you believe that if we pray tonight, Ngozi can walk back in here on Sunday?" she asked. The kids cheered, and then they bowed their heads and prayed for my daughter. I was touched by their precious faith. Ngozi might not have shown improvement, but their prayers strengthened me.

The next morning as I was getting the kids ready for school, five-year-old Ige came up behind me and said, "Mommy, we need to pray for Ngozi right now."

From somewhere inside of me, I received a nudge from the Holy Spirit, telling me that, indeed, we needed to pray *right then*. I was tired, and I was trying to get the kids ready for school. We had been praying for months, and intensely for six days, and nothing had happened. *Lord, why do you want me to pray again now?*

But I called all the kids into the living room, and I said, "Jesus, I'm tired. And I know your plan is to heal Ngozi. Can you do it now?" Something inside of me told me to hold her hands and help her stand. I reached down and took hold of her hands.

As soon as Ngozi realized I was going to help her stand, she said, "No, Mommy, I can't."

"Yes, you can. You're going to walk." I knew it was a foolish thing to say. Her muscles were weak, and her feet were turned inward. Even if she could walk, she would need lots of therapy to correct the position of her feet. But I said it again, "You are going to walk *today*."

Suddenly her foot turned and straightened! I couldn't believe it! The kids stared as I held her hand and she slowly stood up. Suddenly they began to giggle. "Ngozi's getting up!" they shouted.

But Ngozi fell back to the floor. I took her hands again and held them as she once again stood up. This time she stood up on her own. The kids started laughing and jumping up and down. Then Ngozi started walking on her own. Her feet were perfectly straight as she put one foot in front of the other. The kids couldn't contain their excitement; Melvin jumped on the couch as they all shouted and laughed with joy. I cried; I couldn't believe I was seeing her walk! I picked up the phone and called Esther. "She's walking! She's really walking!" I could hear Esther weeping on the other end of the line. I knew it was a miracle. Then I called the church and told them what happened. That Sunday Ngozi walked into kids' church all by herself. Seeing the excitement on the little faces of the children who had prayed so hard was a moment I will never forget.

But my blessings didn't end there. Ngozi had missed almost two months of school, but after she returned, she caught up in no time. She was tested for the gifted program and got accepted into one of the best junior high school programs in Brooklyn. She excelled there, becoming a leader among her peers. When she graduated, she received a check for three hundred dollars! A counselor at her school nominated her for a scholars program, and Ngozi made it to the final thirty kids. She was accepted into Emma Willard, one of the oldest and most prestigious schools for girls, where she got a full scholarship for more than thirty-four thousand dollars a year! Last summer she spent two weeks playing basketball for a leadership program at Earth University in Costa Rica—a girl who once couldn't walk leading others and playing basketball! She now attends St. Lawrence University on a full scholarship.

The other kids are all happy and successful too, but perhaps the biggest changes occurred in me. I no longer work as a nursing assistant; instead I am a paraprofessional in the schools, helping special needs children. At church, while serving in the children's ministry, I was drawn to the ones who needed special attention and had trouble in group settings. Over time I recruited others who came alongside me to start a ministry class for special needs children. Exhausted parents can now feel comfortable leaving their children while they attend services to be refreshed by the Lord.

With a one-to-one ratio of adults to children, we have been able to see many wonderful things happen. One year we acted out the Christmas story, and while his parents watched, a little boy who couldn't speak said his first word: "Hallelujah."

I love those kids. I especially love the ones who are a challenge, because I know they need the Holy Spirit most. Sometimes I call the parents at home, and I say, "I understand what you're going through. I don't know why God healed mine and he didn't heal yours or hasn't healed yours yet. But I'm going to pray with you and support you." The prayers and support of many people got me through those difficult days when I was so tired. Now I have a calling on my life to help others.

One day while I was getting ready to leave church, a woman named Carol who works in Family Ministry, passed by me. As I saw her long braid swinging behind her, I was suddenly reminded of a night long ago. "Carol!" I said.

She turned and looked at me. "Why are you crying, Annes?"

We now knew each other, but I had never made the connection to that night at the prayer meeting. "The Lord just reminded me of something. Do you remember years ago when you gave a woman a twenty-dollar bill?"

"Yes, I certainly do. What happened to that woman? Do you know her?"

By now I was crying so hard I had to choke back my tears to get the words out. "I was that woman."

God answers big prayers, like healing a child, and small prayers, like providing cab fare to get home. Often the Holy Spirit moves other people to help. Now my hope is that I will be an answer to prayer for parents who are tired and struggling to do the best they can for their children.

WE ARE NO LONGER SPECTATORS

Most of us are unaware of a certain event in the Bible that likely changed the history of the Christian church. Understanding what happened in that moment will help us understand more about the Holy Spirit. The story is found in Acts, and the setting was Antioch. After Saul's conversion on the road to Damascus, he moved around a bit, making a short visit to Jerusalem with the apostles before returning to his hometown of Tarsus. Later Barnabas went there and persuaded Saul to join him in helping the church at Antioch where God's grace was so evident (Acts 11:19 – 26). The two of them joined other gifted prophets and teachers, and ministered there for many months, strengthening the believers' faith in Jesus.

Then came the pivotal moment. As the leaders of the church in Antioch were purposely drawing near to God (worshiping and fasting), God drew near to them as promised (see James 4:8). Luke tells the story in a matter-of-fact manner, which gives us some insight into the spiritual practices of early Christian leaders. Possibly they had some prophetic intimation that the Lord was planning changes among them. They tuned their ears to his voice, and God responded.

"While they were worshiping the Lord and fasting, the Holy Spirit said, 'Set apart for me Barnabas and Saul for the work to which I have called them.' So after they had fasted and prayed, they placed their hands on them and sent them off" (Acts 13:2 – 3).

The believers heard the Spirit instruct them to "set apart Barnabas and Saul" so they could be sent out to do some new, specific work for God. We're not sure how that message was delivered. Was it through some prophetic gift of the Spirit? The details are omitted, but it was dramatic and unmistakable. No one seemed particularly surprised by the Spirit's directive for Paul and Barnabas to give themselves to this rather vague calling. The Spirit was revealing his mind, and the church leadership responded. They fasted and prayed some more, placed their hands on the two men, and sent them off (v. 3).

So what's so significant about that moment? That was the beginning of Saul's first missionary journey. His travels changed the entire course of the Christian church. In fact, it was during his first trip that Saul's name was changed to Paul, and he stepped out to take the lead as God used him in even greater ways than his older compatriot Barnabas. From that point on, the book of Acts shifts directions. It is no longer focused on the acts of Peter, James, and John around Jerusalem; instead, it focuses on Paul and his travels. Though he wasn't one of the original apostles, he became the greatest of them all. He also became the ministry model for the Christian leaders through the ages as he preached, taught, and founded churches throughout the world.

Set Apart for an Illogical Calling

When God's Spirit moves, a continual process of setting believers apart and sending them out to work for Christ is set in motion. And it isn't reserved for only those in formal ministry. Sometimes we're asked to leave our house, go down the block, and encourage a hurting neighbor, or maybe to join a ministry in our church to train children. Perhaps we're to go on short-term mission trips or give ourselves to the kind of intercessory prayer that transforms lives. When the Spirit is moving and we yield to his influences, life becomes both exciting and filled with challenges only God can meet. No one is left to be merely a spectator.

The contemporary definition of church seems to leave everything up to the professional clergy while everyone else sits back and watches. But this goes against God's plan that we're all a part of the same body and that he has a specific purpose for each member (1 Cor 12:12 – 27). Christianity shouldn't be reduced to filling our heads with more Bible knowledge that we never act on. It's about hearing the Spirit's call, surrendering to him, and then giving ourselves totally to the work he puts before us. It involves strong efforts, faith to overcome discouragement, and perseverance to keep at it no matter what.

Oddly, God loves to choose the most unlikely, untrained, and imperfect folks to accomplish amazing things. Abraham lied when under pressure, Moses killed a man before he became Israel's deliverer, King David's family dismissed him as only a shepherd boy, and the apostle Peter was a fisherman with no formal religious training. Church history since then gives us countless more examples of this encouraging truth:

> Brothers and sisters, think of what you were when you were called. Not many of you were wise by human standards; not many were influential; not many were of noble birth. But God chose the foolish things of the world to shame the wise; God chose the weak things of the world to shame the strong. God chose the lowly things of this world and the despised things — and the things that are not — to nullify the things that are, so that no one may boast before him. (1 Cor. 1:26 – 29)

Note that those words were written to a congregation of believers in Jesus, not to the clergy. In case you're feeling inadequate and untrained when the Spirit calls, please remember that this is the way God usually works so that he will be guaranteed to receive all the glory.

For God to use ordinary people, hard and firm *human* plans have to give way. What we think is logical, what makes the most sense to us, must always yield to the Holy Spirit's calling.

Consider Philip, the deacon who through the Holy Spirit became an evangelist. He ended up preaching the gospel to large crowds in Samaria, and God brought **For God to use ordinary people, hard and firm *human* plans have to give way.** a spiritual awakening in that city. Although it surely didn't make sense for Philip to leave the crusade he was leading and head out of town to an isolated desert road, that's exactly what an angel of the Lord told him to do (Acts 8:26). While he was there, along came an Ethiopian eunuch (you'll read in a minute why I love Ethiopians so much) who was reading the book of Isaiah in his chariot. "The Spirit told Philip, 'Go to that chariot and stay near it' " (v. 29). While near the chariot, a conversation ensued that permitted Philip to share the gospel and lead the eunuch to Christ.

Notice how the Holy Spirit gave specific, almost trivial directions. "Go to that chariot and stay near it." The Spirit probably said that to Philip, in a still small voice that Philip recognized in his heart. It wasn't an addition to Scripture. It was detailed instructions given by the Holy Spirit to a believer that resulted in the gospel of Jesus spreading to the continent of Africa.

If we insist on doing our own thing in our own time and resist God's "setting apart," we will miss out on the amazing "sent out" part. None of us can possibly know in advance what God wants to do with our lives. Certainly no one ever would have predicted that Saul, the persecutor of the church, would become Paul, the greatest of the apostles.

The Unlikely Evangelist

Paul was Jewish, trained as a Pharisee, and an expert in Old Testament teaching. No one was better equipped to take the good news to the Jewish people. But that's not where God placed Paul. Instead, he used him to spread the gospel among the Gentiles! Logically, Peter would have been a better choice, but God's ways are *not* our ways (Peter became the apostle to the Jews!). When God's Spirit moves, his purposes are revealed and accomplished in ways that no committee, personality test, or computer program could ever figure out.

D. L. Moody is a great example of that. No one ever would have expected him to be one of the greatest evangelists of all time. Moody was initially a shoe salesman and basically uneducated. He was a short, overweight man and not very good-looking. He had a slight speech impediment and a rapid-fire delivery when he spoke. After he became a Christian, he started working with children on the streets of Chicago, working with the YMCA, and later handing out tracts during the Civil War. Though he never went to seminary, his work bore fruit, and eventually he was invited to England to preach.

While he was there, well-trained, velvet-tongued pastors sat in amazement at his preaching. Many of their churches were dead, and the kingdom wasn't being extended. But along came Moody, and the crowds followed. Despite his limitations, God's blessing was evident. The guy couldn't even pronounce Daniel correctly. He said Dan'l. And more difficult names like Nebuchadnezzar? Not even close.

A man known only by Mr. Reynolds once described the first time he met Moody:

> The first meeting I ever saw him at was in a little old shanty that had been abandoned by a saloon-keeper. Mr. Moody had got the place to hold the meeting in at night. I went there a little late: and the first thing I saw was a man standing up, with a few tallow candles around him, holding a negro boy, and trying to read to him the story of the Prodigal Son; and a great many of the words he could not make out, and had to skip. I thought, *If the Lord can ever use such an instrument as that for his honor and glory, it will astonish me.* After that meeting was over, Mr. Moody said to me, "Reynolds, I have got only one talent: I have no education, but I love the Lord Jesus Christ, and I want to do something for Him: and I want you to pray for me." I have never ceased from that day to this, morning and night, to pray for that devoted Christian soldier.[1]

In a sense, Moody was nearly semiliterate. I once saw a letter written by Moody that was reproduced in *Love Them In: The Life and Theology of D. L. Moody*, by Stanley N. Gundry.[2] Any sixth grader could do better. There were no capital letters, and commas and periods were few and far between. He would have been laughed at today when we judge ministry by slickness of delivery style and not by spiritual power. Yet this man preached to millions of people with no sound system and became one of the best-known evangelists in the history of Christianity. He led thousands to the Lord and went on to found three schools and a university.

> **Sometimes God's work encompasses world-changing missions; at other times, it is much more personal and closer to home.**

We're not all called to be a D. L. Moody. But regardless of how we're set apart, it is God's responsibility to equip us. And in the case of Moody, boy, did he ever!

The Spirit calls Christians to all sorts of work for him. Sometimes the work encompasses world-changing missions, such as that of Moody. At other times, the work is much more personal and closer to home.

A Hunger She Couldn't Satisfy

My daughter, Susan, and her husband, Brian, know something about that. Their family was complete. They had a son and daughter who were long out of diapers, but since a visit to Haiti at age seventeen, Susan had felt a recurring tug on her heart to adopt.

She got married young, but because of some physical problems, she was told she probably wouldn't have children, and if she did, there would be lots of complications. But that never happened. She had her first child, Luke, when she was twenty-three, and her daughter, Claire, not long after. But when Claire was five, Susan and Brian wanted to have another child. This time, however, she unexpectedly miscarried.

The miscarriage rekindled her long-held desire to adopt. "In that moment," Susan said, "it almost seemed selfish for me to want more biological children." Brian was open to the idea of adopting, but he wanted to make sure the Spirit was truly leading them.

While Susan and Brian were on a mission trip to the Philippines, one of the locals mentioned that a family had just given birth to a child, but because they couldn't afford to take care of her, they planned to sell her. Susan was all action. "I'll take her!" she said immediately, not understanding anything about international adoption laws.

A friend on the mission trip led Brian and Susan to a remote area where the family lived. Inside the hut was a very sick mother lying with her newborn. The family quickly confirmed they wanted to give up their new baby.

Susan and Brian had no idea that the whole thing was illegal. A lawyer drew up the paperwork, and Susan and Brian paid him and signed the forms. They took the baby girl and named her Emily. They placed her in the care of a couple at the church where they were ministering and promised to be back soon to take Emily home.

But back in the United States, Susan researched adoption law and quickly realized something was wrong. "This is totally illegal!" Susan told Brian. With that, they began a two-year, heartbreaking journey of trying to identify political, legal, and humanitarian connections in both the Philippines and the United States who could help them bring Emily to the United States. But nothing worked.

Eventually everyone began to see that it wasn't going to work for Susan and Brian to bring Emily home. During that time, the family in the Philippines who had cared for Emily had fallen in love with her. They joyously committed to adopting her and raising Emily as their own.

Despite the heartbreak, Susan still felt the tug on her soul to adopt. While she was ready to move forward, Brian was cautious. They had already been through so much.

"It didn't work out with Emily," Brian said one day. "Maybe we're just not supposed to adopt." Susan wanted to honor her husband. She prayed the desire for adoption would go away if they weren't supposed to adopt; but, if anything, it only came back stronger. Something inside of her wouldn't let go of bringing another child into her family.

On the Internet, she learned about a Christian adoption agency with a program in Ethiopia. She talked to Brian about calling them, but he was still apprehensive and wanted to be sure it was what God wanted. After a few weeks of conversation, Susan couldn't wait any longer. "I'm going to call them today and start the process."

That morning, as they both headed to their offices at the Brooklyn Tabernacle, Susan felt torn. "I wanted to call the agency that day, but I also knew Brian wasn't convinced God wanted this. Could he be right? My kids were ten and twelve. And in a lot of ways, I was done. They were self-sufficient, and I was independent again. It had been a long time since I carried a diaper bag."

"What was even crazier was that three years earlier, I had taken over leadership of the Brooklyn Tabernacle children's ministry. Between my work and my kids at home, you would think that I wouldn't want more kids. But my desire to adopt had only grown. A lot of people said to me, 'What are you doing?' And I would think, *I don't know. But as much as the idea alarms you, it delights me.*"

God had put something in Susan's heart, and she couldn't let go. "It was a hunger in me that I couldn't satisfy. I was consumed with the idea." But obviously Brian wasn't there yet.

> **God had put something in Susan's heart, and she couldn't let go.**

Susan was busy in meetings that morning, and it was midafternoon before she had a chance to return to her desk and see a message on her cell phone from Terry, a member of the church.

Terry is a respected woman in our church whom God sometimes uses in the gifts of the Spirit. "I knew of her," Susan said, "but I had never talked to her. I can be cautious of people being used in the gifts of the Spirit, but I always respected Terry. I believe she's the real deal and that she really hears from God." *How did she get my cell phone number?* Susan wondered.

She played the message. "Susan, God has put you on my heart," Terry said. "I've been praying for you all day. I feel like God's given me a word for you, and I'm apprehensive to give it. I want to be careful that this is from God. But this is what I believe he's telling me. He wants to say to you that it won't be long now and just to use wisdom as you proceed."

Susan was stunned. This was the day she was supposed to call the agency, and earlier that day, Brian said he needed to hear from God. That was it. Susan called Brian, "You got your word! You'll never believe what happened." She told him about Terry's phone call. Brian agreed it was the sign he needed, so Susan called the agency and started the process.

They went on the waiting list in August, and then on January 22, they received a call from the agency that a baby boy was waiting for them. They named him Levi. The details of Levi's life were sad. Levi's mom had passed away from malaria while giving birth to her son. Levi's father knew he couldn't take care of his new son in addition to the four children he already had. In the remote area where Levi's family lived, without a mother's milk, Levi would have had little chance for survival.

Some parents who couldn't feed their babies left them to die, but Levi's father wanted more for his son. So that grieving father traveled eight hours on a bus to bring Levi to the orphanage. Weeks later, when Susan, Brian, and their two children arrived in Ethiopia, the father made the same eight-hour trip back to finalize the adoption in court. Through an interpreter, the father told them he hoped Levi would become a doctor and come back to Ethiopia one day with a cure for malaria.

Because those people followed the promptings of the Spirit, I now have the most amazing grandson! On my desk is an 8 x 10 frame with a picture of one-year-old Levi. I love his handsome face and the mischievous twinkle in his dark brown eyes. When he walks into a room, people notice the light within him.

I believe it was the Holy Spirit who inspired Susan all those years ago and continually stirred the idea of adoption so she couldn't let it go. Terry would tell you it was the prompting of the Holy Spirit that made her call Susan and leave a message that day even though she felt uncomfortable and wasn't sure why she did it. And Brian felt peace only after the Spirit's confirmation. It was also the prompting of the Holy Spirit that led Levi's father to make that long journey to place his baby in the caring hands of adoption workers.

The Holy Spirit worked through many people over many years to bring Levi to our family. And though Levi is a special joy, Susan would tell you that he hasn't made her life easier. Brian is an incredibly busy associate pastor in our church. They have two other children and live in the greater New York City area — a difficult place to raise a family. But Susan would also tell you that God puts us in hard places so that we become more dependent on him and so we can experience his power in greater ways. What the Spirit leads us to do isn't always easy, and it doesn't always make a lot of sense, but whom God calls, he equips. And in this case, I am so glad he did! After all, I'm the only Polish-Ukrainian pastor in downtown Brooklyn with an Ethiopian grandson.

Prompt Responses

When God sets us apart and sends us out, it isn't necessarily to preach or be a missionary. There are countless examples of people in our churches whom the Holy Spirit has called to start a new ministry, evangelize in the streets, disciple and care for senior citizens, teach the Bible to preteens, or serve his people in many other ways. Just as each member of the human body functions differently from the others, the Spirit energizes each of us in the body of Christ to fulfill God's purpose. Without the Spirit's power being exercised, we tend to sit on the sidelines, inactive and unfulfilled. Worse, we are tempted to critique those actually "in the game" trying to proclaim Christ and serve his people. Anyone can criticize the efforts of another believer, but at the judgment seat of Christ, we will answer for ourselves only, not another.

Although God can speak to anyone at any time, if we want to discover what he has called us to do, we would do well to remember the "drawing near" of the leaders in Antioch. They were "worshiping the Lord" and denying themselves food for a season so they could become more spiritually sensitive to the Spirit of God. Somehow the Spirit actually named Barnabas and Saul. He had been tracking their growth and yieldedness through the years. As they sought the Lord in prayer, the Spirit revealed a new work assignment for them that would result in awesome blessings to countless people. This was not a case of two men hearing strange voices that no one else could confirm. Barnabas and Saul had the leadership of the church bear witness to the Spirit's call. When the Holy Spirit speaks and leads, confirmation will always come in some way, including by the witness of other mature believers.

Christ didn't die on the cross so that we would spend our time as Christians on earth merely sitting around waiting for his return. Jesus said, "The harvest is plentiful but the workers are few" (Matt. 9:37). The reason for the shortage today is that too few are yielded to the Spirit whom Christ sent to us. But there's still time, and we have a patient, merciful Savior on our side.

Who knows how God can use you if you step out in faith and let the Holy Spirit take control? We're not called to be spectators watching from the stands as the prince of darkness goes about to steal, kill, and destroy (John 10:10). Jesus said there is a shortage of workers, but the actual work will be done by God's Spirit through *you and me* doing things beyond our wildest imagination. It all begins when you offer yourself to serve.

And then we can pray the prophet Isaiah's prayer, "Here am I. Send me!" (Isa. 6:8).

WHERE DO WE GO FROM HERE?

Sometimes I wonder what it must have been like for the Israelites to have the presence of God in their midst — dwelling among them and guiding them as they traveled from Egypt to the Promised Land. Though Moses was the only one who got to talk directly to God, all of the Israelites could see a manifestation of God's presence — the pillar of cloud by day and the pillar of fire by night.

The pillars first appeared as the Hebrews were nearing the Red Sea. Later Moses received the Ten Commandments from God on Mount Sinai. Along with the moral instructions, he also received detailed instructions on how the Israelites should worship God. Using the plans Moses brought back, the Israelites built a tabernacle. This tabernacle was a portable temple or temporary structure that could be packed up and taken with them as they moved around the desert. Then whenever they stopped, the tabernacle was set up in the middle of the camp. The tabernacle served as the focal point for priestly worship and sacrifices offered up to God.

Behind the Holy Place, where only the priests ministered daily, was a place called the Holy of Holies, a special room that only the high priest could enter and only once a year on the Day of Atonement. In that room resided the ark of the covenant, a sacred, gold-covered trunk also built to the specifications that God gave Moses. The cover was solid gold and called the mercy seat. Inside the ark were the stone tablets, on which were written the Ten Commandments.

After the tabernacle was set up for the first time, an awesome event happened. "[A] cloud covered the tent of meeting, and the glory of the LORD filled the tabernacle" (Ex. 40:34). But that cloud covering was anything but ordinary — it was literally God's presence in some mysterious form. The God of Israel had come to settle among his people above the ark of the covenant. This was such an extraordinary moment that "Moses could not enter the tent of meeting because the cloud had settled on it, and the glory of the LORD filled the tabernacle" (Ex. 40:35). But God did more than come into their midst; he used his presence as a way to guide them. When the cloud lifted from above the tabernacle and moved forward, the Israelites packed up camp and followed. God didn't tell them to "go." He went first and told them to "follow." When the cloud stopped, so did the Israelites.

"In all the travels of the Israelites, whenever the cloud lifted from above the tabernacle, they would set out; but if the cloud did not lift, they did not set out.... So the cloud of the LORD was over the tabernacle by day, and fire was in the cloud by night, in the sight of all the Israelites during all their travels" (Ex. 40:36 – 38).

Think of how marvelous this must have been! God had given them moral commandments reflecting his holiness; he had given them a sacrificial system of offerings for sin; but now he had given them *his actual presence*.

The cloud must have greatly reassured the Israelites. It reminded them that God was there — that he was guiding and protecting them. They were not like the Philistines, Amorites, or other Canaanite peoples. They were the chosen people of the true and living God, whose presence dwelt among them. Imagine how horror-stricken they would have been if one day they woke up and didn't see the cloud. Imagine the chaos and panic that would have ensued if the cloud of glory, the very presence of God, was no longer with them.

Why have we settled for anemic Christian living when the living Spirit of God is available for the asking?

But that's exactly what happened. One day, in fact, the cloud was no longer there. We don't know when the cloud went away or why there was no longer a visible sign of God's presence. The Bible doesn't tell us any of those details. I can't help but wonder what happened. Did God leave because they turned away from obeying him? Did people even notice the cloud was missing? If they did, did they care? Did they do anything to get him back?

Missing in Action

In this book, we have studied the activity, power, and presence of the Holy Spirit in the early Christian church. When we consider the movement of the Spirit and the great work accomplished for Christ in the early church and compare it to our lives and congregations today, it's hard not to wonder what happened. Why have we settled for anemic Christian living and lifeless church routines when the living Spirit of God is available for the asking?

A strong word of rebuke from God to his own people is found in the writings of Jeremiah. Could it still apply to many of us today?

> Hear the word of the LORD, you descendants of Jacob,
>   all you clans of Israel.
>
> This is what the LORD says:
>
> "What fault did your ancestors find in me,
>   that they strayed so far from me?
> They followed worthless idols
>   and became worthless themselves.
> They did not ask, 'Where is the LORD,
>   who brought us up out of Egypt
> and led us through the barren wilderness,
>   through a land of deserts and ravines,
> a land of drought and utter darkness,
>   a land where no one travels and no one lives?'"
>
> *Jeremiah 2:4 – 6, emphasis added*

Israel had lost the blessing and presence of their God, and amazingly, no one seemed to care. Despite God's powerful work on their behalf in the past, no one had the spiritual courage and discernment to ask, "Where is the Lord?" Their idolatry and other sins had grieved and then forfeited God's presence, but the real tragedy was that no one missed him. Temple worship continued and animal sacrifices were offered exactly as Moses commanded, but the Spirit of God had long since gone.

Could that be happening today? Hymns and praise choruses are sung; a sound doctrinal sermon is preached; our church services are timed and orchestrated perfectly. Too often, however, there is little of the presence of God that produces awe, conviction of sin, overflowing joy, and life-transforming ministry. We can easily settle for "church" instead of God. And every succeeding generation shaped in that mold makes it harder for anyone to dare ask, "Where is the Lord?"

But there's another prophetic passage that brings hope to all of us who hunger for a spiritual breakthrough in our lives, churches, and nation:

> Then his people recalled the days of old,
>   the days of Moses and his people —
> *where is he* who brought them through the sea,
>   with the shepherd of his flock?
> Where is he who
>   set his Holy Spirit among them?
>   *Isaiah 63:11, emphasis added*

That passage speaks of a day when God's people will remember the past. They will remember how the Lord intervened on their behalf and his presence was glorious among them. Inspired by those memories, they will cry out, "Where is he who set his Holy Spirit among us?" Then even stronger petitions will go up to the Lord, "Oh, that you would rend the heavens and come down, that the mountains would tremble before you!" (Isa. 64:1).

This desperate prayer has marked every spiritual revival God ever granted. Believers sense their loss and can't settle any longer for merely going to church. They must have God *himself* filling their lives.

Before Israel settled in Canaan, Moses got to the heart of the matter when he pleaded with God for more help to lead the people. "The Lord replied, 'My Presence will go with you, and I will give you rest.' Then Moses said to him, "If your Presence does not go with us, do not send us up from here. How will anyone know that you are pleased with me and with your people unless you go with us? What else will distinguish me and your people from all the other people on the face of the earth?" (Ex. 33:14 – 16).

How astounding is Moses' prayer! Especially when compared to our satisfaction with far less than the best God has to offer. Moses told the Lord not even to send them toward the Promised Land unless he was with them. How else would others know God's approval of Moses and Israel if there was no glorious presence?

This distinguishing mark made the Hebrews different from all other peoples on the earth — not their weapons, victory songs, or past experiences. The presence of the Lord set them apart as God's covenant nation. In the same way, the early church not only rejoiced in the fact that the Spirit was given, but they also coveted the manifestation of his presence among them. Their goal was to see unbelievers visiting their services and leaving filled with awe and declaring, "God is really among you" (1 Cor. 14:24 – 25).

Without the Spirit, Christianity is reduced to head knowledge *about* God, empty traditions, and a social club mentality. We need to ask God to give us a fresh revelation of what *his church* was meant to look like. Without that proper foundation, we'll end up building on sand. But with it we will see seasons of spiritual renewal from the Holy Spirit that produce amazingly fruitful evangelism and a growing atmosphere of love among believers.

How to Get There from Here

Where do we go from here, and how do we get there? We must start where miracles almost always begin: with acknowledgment and confession. If we are far from God and how he wants things to be, we can't live in denial or with pride-serving rationalizations. Whether for us personally or our congregations, we must ask Jesus for an accurate reading of our spiritual temperature. Do we have a lukewarm faith? Long ago Christ gave a temperature reading to seven churches (Rev. 2 – 3), and he will also be faithful in love to show us where we have failed him. No matter how far we have drifted or fallen, he will bring us back to wholeness and spiritual vitality if we permit him. But it must start with our sincere, humble acknowledgment that we need help from the Holy Spirit. We must confess that openly to the Lord.

> We need to ask God to give us a fresh revelation of what *his church* was meant to look like.

We must also give ourselves to fellowship with God in prayer and serious study of his Word. The Bible will help us pray in faith, and prayer will help us understand the words of Scripture. As we trust God, he will help us manage our time and grant us self-discipline. Then, as new light dawns in our souls, we will be compelled to confess and forsake every sin and ungodly habit. True repentance will turn us away from selfish indulgence and toward God. We will come broken and weak before him, but the important fact is, we will come.

Will God reject our requests for his help because we're still flawed and immature in some ways? Not if we desire to live right before God and experience more of the Holy Spirit. Humility and a sincere desire to please him will always gain a hearing at the throne of grace. We must not keep on looking inward at our faults and moral failures. Let's just sincerely confess everything the Spirit shows us and then move on to better things, like always keeping our eyes on Jesus (Heb. 12:2). He is the one who promised the Holy Spirit to men who had recently deserted him at a critical time. It wasn't their track record or righteousness that earned the promise; it was his love and their desperate need.

Does the Spirit want to do everything we have read about or not? If he doesn't, then the Bible is a very misleading book. If he does, then our seeking his help, strength, love, wisdom, and direction is not in vain. Each time the Holy Spirit prompts us to move in a new direction, let's obey immediately. This will help us develop a deeper sensitivity to his voice.

And as we must wait for fresh visitations from the Spirit, let us remain patient. As sure as morning follows night, the Holy Spirit *will* move in new ways among us. Let's leave the timing and manifestation of those things to God, whose ways are not like ours. But while we wait, let us keep working for Christ and serving others in his name. Spiritual revival is not reserved for hermits hidden away in a desert, but for believers living in the real world. With God the best is always yet to come.

The Spirit has moved in the past and accomplished extraordinary things that glorified Jesus and extended his kingdom. But the world has never been darker, more violent, or hungrier for something that satisfies the soul. Jesus is the answer, and we are the Master's messengers on a mission. He knew what our needs would be and sent the Holy Spirit to help us over every mountain and through every difficult valley. The Holy Spirit cannot be contained in a box; he works like the wind. He blows where he wants to, and he manifests himself through people in ways of his own choosing.

When the Spirit works through surrendered, faith-filled people like you and me, Christ will be glorified. The church will be built up. The Word of God will be honored. The kingdom of God will be extended.

For that is why he came.

NOTES

Chapter 1: Holy Disruptions

1. Sabrina Tavernise, "Hate Engulfs Christians in Pakistan," *New York Times*, August 2, 2009, http://www.nytimes.com/2009/08/03/world/asia/03pstan.html.

Chapter 3: Christianity Is Hopeless without the Spirit

1. http://www.raptureready.com/resource/chadwick/chadwick30.html.
2. R. A. Torrey, *Power-Filled Living: How to Receive God's Best for Your Life* (New Kensington, Pa.: Whitaker House, 1998), 151.
3. William Booth, *Salvation Soldiery: A Series of Addresses on the Requirements of Jesus Christ's Service* (London: International Headquarters, 1890), 141.

Chapter 4: Controlled by the Spirit

1. Torrey, *Power-Filled Living*, 225; italics in original.
2. Charles G. Finney, *Revival Lectures* (Grand Rapids: Fleming H. Revell, 1995).

Chapter 6: The Word Comes Alive

1. *The Word: The Bible from 26 Translations*, ed. Curtis Vaughan (Gulfport, Miss.: Mathis, 1988), 2124.

2. William Law, *Power of the Spirit: Selections from the Writings of William Law*, ed. Andrew Murray (Bloomington, Minn.: Bethany Fellowship, 1977), 96.

Chapter 7: There Are Signs and Symbols of Renewal
1. Quotation from NIV 1984 edition.

Chapter 8: There Is Joy
1. Quotation from NIV 1984 edition.

Chapter 13: We Love the Unlovable
1. Quotation from NIV 1984 edition.
2. Quotation from NIV 1984 edition.
3. Quotation from NIV 1984 edition.

Chapter 14: We Are Drawn into Fellowship
1. Author unknown, *Crumbs for the Lord's Little Ones*, I (London, 1853), 205, http://books.google.com/books?pg=PR1&id=HmEEA AAAQAAJ#v=onepage&q&f=false.

Chapter 17: We Can Shake the Kingdom with Our Prayers
1. Samuel Chadwick, *The Path of Prayer*, http://www.raptureready. com/resource/chadwick/chadwick1.html.
2. Charles G. Finney, *Lectures on Revivals of Religion*, 2nd ed. (New York: Leavitt, Lord & Co., 1835), http://www.whatsaiththescripture.com/Voice/Revival.Lectures.2.html.
3. Quotation from NIV 1984 edition.
4. Chadwick, *Path of Prayer*, http://www.raptureready.com/resource/chadwick/chadwick7.html.

Chapter 19: We Are No Longer Spectators
1. Edgar Johnson Goodspeed, *A Full History of the Wonderful Career of Moody and Sankey, in Great Britain and America* (London, Ont.: John O. Robinson, 1876), 25, http://books.google.com/books?id=TqgMAAAAIAAJ&dq=career%20of%20Moody%20and%20Sankey&pg=PA25#v=onepage&q&f=false.
2. Stanley N. Gundry, *Love Them In: The Life and Theology of D. L. Moody* (Chicago: Moody, 1999).

When God's Spirit Moves
Participant's Guide with DVD

Jim Cymbala with Dean Merrill

Pack containing one softcover guide and one DVD. What happens when the Holy Spirit moves in a church? In this six-session DVD study with participant's guide, you will learn not only about the person of the Holy Spirit, but also:

- How to make room for the work of the Spirit in your life and in your church
- How the Spirit empowers you to be creative and honor God with your gifts and talents
- How to listen in prayer and apply the Word of God
- How the Spirit is active in the work of healing your body, your emotions, and your relationships
- How your personal transformation leads to greater transformations in your community and around the world through the changed lives of believers
- How your church can become a place where the message of the gospel is heard and people experience the life-giving power of a grace-filled community

Pastor and bestselling author Jim Cymbala will show you how to infuse a fresh sense of God's power in your church and in your life as a follower of Jesus.

Pack: 978-0-310-88942-7

Available in stores and online!

When God's People Pray

Six Sessions on the Transforming Power of Prayer

Jim Cymbala, Bestselling Author of Fresh Wind, Fresh Fire

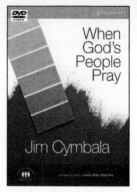

Prayer can change lives and circumstances like nothing else can. What are the keys that unlock its power, that turn prayer from a mere activity into a vital link with God and all his resources? In this DVD, Jim Cymbala, pastor of Brooklyn Tabernacle, shows you and your small group truths about prayer that God has used to turn his own church from a tiny, struggling inner-city congregation into a vital, thriving community of believers who pray with passion, focus, and faith.

Featuring teachings by Jim Cymbala and video interviews of ordinary people who have received extraordinary answers to their prayers, these six sessions will help you pray with new confidence.

Six sessions

1. God's Heart for Us
2. The Amazing Power of Prayer
3. Obedience in Prayer
4. The Word of God and Prayer
5. Why Prayer Matters
6. Creating a Prayer Ministry in Your Church

DVD-ROM: 978-0-310-26735-5

Available in stores and online!